ALL-PRO HOCKEY
83-84

BRIAN McFARLANE

Scholastic-TAB Publications Ltd.
123 Newkirk Road, Richmond Hill, Ontario,
Canada

We gratefully acknowledge the following people and teams for permission to use the photographs on the pages indicated:

Steve Babineau, 5; Boston Bruins, 43; Buffalo Sabres, 46,87; Calgary Flames, 37; Chicago Black Hawks,13,90; Bill Cunningham, 34; Detroit Red Wings, 25; Hartford Whalers, 55,99; Los Angeles Kings, 40; Brian McFarlane, 81; Minnesota North Stars, 16; Montreal Canadiens, 49,64,104; Mummery/Strong Photographers, 28,76,83,96,108; New Jersey Devils, 70; New York Islanders, 11,61,93; New York Rangers, 67,102; Philadelphia Flyers, 58; Pittsburgh Penguins, 73; Québec Nordiques, 52; St. Louis Blues, 22; Robert Shaver, 9,19; Washington Capitals, 64; Winnipeg Jets, 31.

Cover photograph copyright © Miles S. Nadal/Masterfile

1st printing 1983   **Printed in Canada**

Manufactured by Webcom Limited

Hockey has a new look in the 80's. There's more emphasis on what I call hockey's three S's—skating, shooting and stickhandling. There's less emphasis on rough play, fighting and intimidation.

Ten years ago NHL teams recruited big, brawny players who tried to punch and pummel their way to the Stanley Cup. But the Montreal Canadiens, some of the European teams, and more recently the Islanders and the Oilers, convinced hockey men that fast, clean hockey with emphasis on individual skills and exciting team play is the key to success.

This approach is good news for the skilled smaller player. Stricter rules governing fighting and rough play keep the bullies on the sidelines or in the penalty box. Parents who might have been tempted to steer their sons and daughters into less rugged games allow their kids to enjoy the thrills that hockey provides.

You don't have to be big and tough to play hockey. The brightest stars in the NHL—players like Wayne Gretzky, Mike Bossy, Denis Savard and Marcel Dionne—learned to play by the rules of the game. Their skills are admired, their talents appreciated by those who watch and cheer.

You'll meet many of hockey's greatest players in the pages ahead. I hope you enjoy reading about them.

Brian McFarlane

HIGHLIGHTS OF THE 1982-83 SEASON IN REVIEW

Pre-season:

The Boston Bruins, with first pick in the entry draft, select defenceman Gord Kluzak. The North Stars take forward Brian Bellows second and the Toronto Maple Leafs choose defenceman Gary Nyland third.

Montreal trades Brian Engblom, Rod Langway, Craig Laughlin and Doug Jarvis to Washington in return for Ryan Walter and Rick Green. The Habs also deal Doug Risebrough to Calgary for a third-round draft choice in 1984 and a switch of second-round choices in 1983.

Colorado moves to New Jersey and joins the Patrick Division as the Devils. Winnipeg moves into the Smythe Division.

New coaches include Bob Johnston in Calgary, Nick Polano in Detroit, Orval Tessier in Chicago and Larry Kish in Hartford.

October:

On October 23 in Vancouver, Boston Bruin forward Norman Leveille suffers a career-ending brain hemmorhage during a game between the Canucks and the Bruins.

November:

Victor Nechaev, a Soviet player living in Los Angeles, becomes the first Soviet to score a goal in the NHL. He is later released by the Kings.

December:

Wayne Gretzky's 30-game point-scoring streak ends in Los Angeles.

The Soviet national team opens its Canadian tour in Edmonton. The Oilers win 4-3.

In the second game of the tour Quebec's Mario Marois breaks his leg trying to check a Soviet player. The Soviets beat Quebec 3-0 and follow up with a 5-0 trouncing of the Montreal Canadiens. Soviet goalie Vladislav Tretiak says he'd like to play with Montreal some day.

Emile Francis turns over the coaching reins of the St. Louis Blues to Barc Plager. There are rumours that the Blues may be sold to a group from Saskatoon.

Things pick up for Toronto when the Leafs acquire Dan Daoust and Gaston Gingras in a trade with Montreal.

Washington sets a team record by going 14 games without a loss.

January:

The Boston Bruins lose Terry O'Reilly for the season with ligament and cartilage damage in the knee.

The Black Hawks give up on Tony Tanti, their number-one draft choice in 1981. Tanti is traded to Vancouver for Curt Fraser.

Glen Sonmor quits as coach of the North Stars and is replaced by Murray Oliver.

Darryl Sittler collects his 1000th career point in Philadelphia. Marcel Dionne scores his 500th career goal.

Only one official, linesman Ron Foyt, shows up for a game in Hartford (the other two were caught in a blizzard) so Mickey Volcan of the Whalers and Garry Howatt of the Devils help Foyt officiate at the hockey game. Foyt referees; the players act as linesmen.

Marcel Dionne

February:

Coach Larry Kish is dismissed by Hartford. Larry Pleau takes over.

Vancouver goalie John Garrett substitutes for injured teammate Richard Brodeur in the all-star game. It appears Garrett will be MVP of the game and win a new car...until Gretzky scores a record four goals in the third period.

The Rangers and the North Stars team up to score a record three goals in 15 seconds. Scorers are Pavelich, Greschner and Plett.

Goalie Pete Peeters' bid for a record undefeated streak ends at 31 games in Buffalo. Peeters falls one game short of the record of 32 held by his coach Gerry Cheevers.

March:

Mark Pavelich ties a Ranger club scoring record with five goals in one game. Rangers beat Hartford 11-3.

General Manager Baz Bastien of Pittsburgh is killed in an auto accident.

Marcel Dionne becomes the first player ever to reach 100 points for seven straight seasons.

Hartford's Larry Pleau gives the Whaler coaching job to John Cuniff.

The Stastny brothers sign new contracts with the Quebec Nordiques. Mike Gartner of Washington recovers from a serious eye injury.

Mike Bossy scores his 50th goal to become the only NHL player to score 50 or more goals in his first six years in the league.

April:

Wayne Gretzky wins the individual scoring title for third straight year. He tallies a record 125 assists.

Mike Bossy finishes the season with 60 goals, marking the first time a player has scored 60 or more in three straight seasons.

Edmonton Oilers score a league record number of goals: 424.

THE TROPHY WINNERS

The NHL employed a new format in naming its award winners in 1983. Two finalists were named in each category. Members of the Professional Hockey Writers' Association did the voting, except for the Vezina Trophy. That award, for the best goal tender, was decided by the 21 general managers.

Hart Trophy
(most valuable player)

Wayne Gretzky (Edmonton)
Pete Peeters (Boston)

Norris Trophy
(best defenceman)

Rod Langway (Washington)
Mark Howe (Philadelphia)

Calder Trophy
(best rookie)

Steve Larmer (Chicago)
Phil Housley (Buffalo)

Selke Trophy
(best defensive forward)

Bobby Clarke (Philadelphia)
Jari Kurri (Edmonton)

Lady Byng Trophy
(gentlemanly conduct, sportsmanship and playing ability)

Mike Bossy (Islanders)
Rick Middleton (Boston)

Vezina Trophy
(best goalie)

Pete Peeters (Boston)
Roland Melanson (Islanders)

Mike Bossy

OTHER WINNERS

Orval Tessier, Chicago

Named Coach of the Year for guiding his team to fourth place in the overall standings in his rookie season. Bryan Murray of Washington was a close second in the voting.

Lanny McDonald, Calgary

Winner of the Bill Masterton Trophy for perseverance, sportsmanship and dedication to hockey.

Charlie Huddy, Edmonton

Winner of the Emery Edge Award as the top plus-minus player. Huddy was plus 62.

Wayne Gretzky, Edmonton

Winner of the Art Ross Trophy as leading scorer with 196 points. Winner of a new car as the NHL-Toyota player of the year.

Billy Smith and
Roland Melanson, Islanders

Winners of the William Jennings Award for the goalie or goalies having played a minimum of 25 games for the team with the fewest goals scored against it.

Billy Smith, Islanders

Winner of the Conn Smythe Trophy for Most Valuable Player in the playoffs.

Billy Smith

CHICAGO
BLACK HAWKS

New coach Orval Tessier got the best out of the Chicago Black Hawks last season, producing several new club records. Denis Savard broke his own team scoring record with 120 points, rookie Steve Larmer set a goal-scoring mark for Chicago right wingers with 43 and the Hawks scored a team record of 338 goals. But the statistic that pleased Tessier the most was the goals-against total: 268.

"That's 95 goals fewer than the year before," said Tessier proudly. "That's what I call progress."

Some of the Hawks may not like Tessier's ways; he sometimes snarls at them publicly. But they have to admit he gets results. There's been a rebirth of interest in hockey in Chicago and it's all because the Hawks are winning again.

Denis Savard

STRENGTHS: Tony Esposito and Murray Bannerman played well in goal last season, but Esposito is the oldest player in the league and can't go on forever. Savard is the second-best centre in hockey, Al Secord a great goal scorer (54 last season) and rookie of the year Larmer a dandy winger. There's good depth on this club, too, and lots of experience. Doug Wilson is an all-star defenceman and the Hawks are a disciplined crew with a splendid power play, even though it fizzled in the playoffs.

WEAKNESSES: In last spring's playoffs against Edmonton the Hawks seemed to lose some of their enthusiasm and drive. Problems between coach and players may hurt the Hawks. Tessier's harsh criticism, such as his call for "18 heart transplants" during the series with Edmonton, irritates the players. His blowups have earned him the nickname "Mount Orval."

THE FUTURE: Ken Yaremchuk, the Hawks' number-one draft choice in 1982, may find a spot at centre. Jerome Dupont, a large defenceman drafted from the Toronto Marlies in 1980, has had two years of minor league play to improve his skills, while Behn Wilson, acquired in a trade with Philadelphia, will bring toughness to the Hawk blueline. The Hawks' first choice in the June entry draft was defenceman Bruce Cassidy of the Ottawa 67s. He may have to be patient despite his 111 points last season in junior hockey.

14

MINNESOTA NORTH STARS

In 1982 General Manager Lou Nanne thought his Minnesota North Stars were on a par with the New York Islanders, a team he considered to be the best in hockey. During the regular season—when the Stars were good, but never great—Nanne knew he'd rated his team too highly. He realized they needed an overhaul when they barely won a first-round playoff match with Toronto and then were outgunned by Chicago in the Norris Division finals. At the end of last season the Stars appeared to be confused, disoriented and devoid of confidence. The new coach, Bill Mahoney, is expected to solve some of the problems. He'll likely demand a more disciplined approach.

Bobby Smith

STRENGTHS: Goal tending is excellent with Gilles Meloche and Don Beaupré sharing the duties. Craig Hartsburg is a defensive gem and Gordie Roberts never gets the attention he deserves. And watch Brian Bellows take over the leader's role on the team. He was the Stars' best player in the second half last year and scored 35 goals as a rookie. Plenty of scoring from players like Broten (32 goals), Smith (24 goals), McCarthy (28 goals), Ciccarelli (37 goals) and Payne (30 goals) are further proof of the team's strength. The Stars boast a potent power play and steady penalty killing.

WEAKNESSES: Lack of team effort is a real problem with the North Stars and there is often too much confusion inside their blueline. The playoffs indicated an inability to produce under pressure and a resulting loss of poise. A dearth of leadership may be remedied by Bellows and Mahoney.

THE FUTURE: Brian Lawton may be a year away from NHL stardom but as the player selected number one in the entry draft he is a first-class centre. He scored 89 goals in 43 games over two seasons at Mount St. Charles prep school in Providence. Lawton was impressive with the U.S. team in the B pool of the World Championships in Japan. He's the only U.S. player ever selected first in the annual draft of amateur talent. Ex-Providence College star Randy Velischek should help on defence and Mike Sands is a top goal tending prospect.

TORONTO
MAPLE LEAFS

The Maple Leafs are excited about the future.
Midway through last season the pieces began to
fit together and by the playoffs the Leafs had a
team that made Nervous Nellies out of their
playoff opponents, the Minnesota North Stars.
The Stars won the post-season battle, but not
without a fight. The Leafs could be the surprise
team of the 1983-84 season.

"The coaches stuck with us and we're going to
justify their faith in us," said Leaf captain Rick
Vaive. "This team has heart, determination and
guts."

John Anderson

STRENGTHS: One of the Leafs' best players is an acrobatic goal tender named Palmateer, who flips and flops in front of most pucks. Borje Salming makes a fine anchor for defence and young Gary Nyland has already shown why he's about to become one of hockey's finest young defencemen. Dan Daoust, a little sparkplug obtained from Montreal last season, along with energetic performers like Walt Poddubny, Peter Ihnacak, Miroslav Frycer and John Anderson, add credence to Rick Vaive's assessment of the team. In short, the Leafs have a good blend of talent.

WEAKNESSES: There is still a lack of depth on the blueline and on the wings. The Leafs were just average on the power play and in killing penalties last season. Playing on home ice in Toronto often puts added pressure on the young players.

THE FUTURE: Looks good. Number-one draft choice Russ Courtnall has great speed and excellent playmaking ability. He scored 36 goals and 61 assists in 60 games last season, missing 13 games because of a broken wrist. Ken Wreggett, drafted in '82, is rated the best junior goalie in the West and Alan Bester of Brantford is the top goalie in the OHL. Defenceman Gary Leeman, drafted in '82, is ready for the NHL, and college star Rich Costello (obtained from the Flyers in the Sittler deal) may join the Leafs after the Olympics.

ST. LOUIS
BLUES

The last few months have been filled with frustration for the St. Louis Blues. Last January came the startling news that the Blues might be sold to a Saskatoon group. Coach Barclay Plager said, "The uncertainty of the move to Saskatoon bothered us a lot. It was always there and it hurt us." In May the NHL governors voted down Saskatoon's bid for the Blues by 15-3 and in July the Blues were sold to a group headed by Harry Ornest, an Edmonton native who now lives in California.

Blues captain Brian Sutter refused to use the possibility of a franchise shift as an excuse for the Blues' poor season. St. Louis finished fourth in the Norris Division with a 25-40-15 mark. "There's no excuse for our dismal season," said Sutter. "We just didn't want to win as much as the guys on the other teams did."

Bernie Federko

STRENGTHS: The goal-scoring and leadership of Sutter (46 goals) along with the excellent playmaking of team scoring leader Bernie Federko (84 points) were outstanding last year. For three seasons Jorgen Pettersson has never scored less than 35 goals while Perry Turnbull is a consistent 30-goal scorer. Joe Mullen, injured much of last season, should be good for 30 goals or more, and Rob Ramage is a high-scoring defenceman.

WEAKNESSES: Overworked netminder Mike Liut (68 games) has slipped a bit in the past two seasons. In fairness to Mike, he needs more help from his defencemen, none of whom is an all-star. There's also a lack of depth up front and a need for a winning attitude. If more of the Blues had Brian Sutter's spirit and will to win there'd be less frustration in St. Louis.

THE FUTURE: The entry draft is the key to every NHL club's success. Two years ago the Blues traded two first-round draft choices for defenceman Rob Ramage, then in June they created history by failing to participate in the draft. Former Cornwall star Doug Gilmour is a top prospect but the future of the Blues lies with last season's rookies Perry Anderson, Mark Reeds, Alain Vigneault and Alain Lemieux.

DETROIT
RED WINGS

Before you can mould a winner on the ice, you must find a winning combination off the ice. The Red Wings feel that new owner Mike Ilitch, new General Manager Jim Devellano and new Coach Nick Polano are cornerstones in the rebuilding of a once-great franchise.

After one season together and despite the fact that the Wings missed the playoffs, there's optimism in the Wings' front office. "Jimmy Devellano is turning this team in the right direction," says Polano. "Hopefully, I'll still be coaching here when we're a really good club in two or three years." A major off-season deal brought glamour-boy Ron Duguay, hard-nosed winger Eddie Johnstone and veteran goal tender Eddie Mio from New York.

Ron Duguay

STRENGTHS: The Wings have a solid defender in Reed Larson. John Ogrodnik is an exceptional scorer (41 goals last season) and Captain Danny Gare provides strong leadership. If Duguay gets over the shock of leaving Broadway he could be a key man for the Wings, and Mio is coming off a fine season.

WEAKNESSES: With a lack of speed and mobility on defence, some of last year's veterans gone and inexperience on the part of the young players, the Red Wings will have big problems. Goal tending has been inconsistent, but Polano is hoping Mio will solve that problem. Corrado Micalef or Greg Stefan will snatch the number two job. Duguay's unhappiness at being traded may show up in his play.

THE FUTURE: Gord Gallant, who played left wing on a line with junior Pat La-Fontaine in Verdun, has the size and toughness the Wings are looking for. Murray Craven, who played a few games for Detroit last season and wasn't quite prepared for the gruelling life of a pro, may be able to handle the job this season. The Red Wings are also taking a close look at the European market, but most of the best talent has already been picked over by other NHL teams.

EDMONTON
OILERS

The Edmonton Oilers have arrived as a major
NHL power. The signs of future greatness were
obvious in the spring of '81 when the upstart
Oilers, with five players still eligible for junior
hockey, eliminated Montreal and pushed the New
York Islanders to six games before losing in the
next playoff round.

The following year the Oilers zoomed to 111
points and second place overall, only to be eliminated early by the Los Angeles Kings. Last season the team matured, finishing tied with Philadelphia for second place overall. The Oilers scored
a record 424 goals and breezed through three
playoff series with Winnipeg, Calgary and Chicago.

In the Stanley Cup finals, the New York Islanders surprised the Oilers with a four-game
sweep of the series.

Paul Coffey

STRENGTHS: Edmonton has strength everywhere. Andy Moog is one of the best young goalies in hockey. Paul Coffey is a superstar and the other defencemen have made penetration of the Oilers' blueline a risky business. Gretzky is Gretzky (71 goals and 196 points) and the supporting cast up front is outstanding. Mark Messier, Glenn Anderson and Jari Kurri each topped 45 goals and Ken Linesman had 33. The Oilers boast the NHL's best power play and there is plenty of depth with good kids waiting for a chance to play.

WEAKNESSES: Surely there's a weakness somewhere in the Oiler machine. The Oilers gave up 315 goals, almost 100 more than Boston's league-leading 228, so the defence could be tighter, and the team was ninth in penalty killing. But chinks in the Oiler armor are difficult to find.

THE FUTURE: The Oilers drafted an outstanding young defenceman last June in Jeff Beukeboom from the Sault Ste. Marie juniors. Beukeboom, like all the other Oiler hopefuls, will have to wait for a chance to play—the current Oilers feel they can look after the future. Top prospects include Marc Habscheid, Olympic team member Gord Shervan and U.S. college player Paul Houck.

WINNIPEG JETS

The Winnipeg Jets stepped into faster company last season, the tough Smythe Division, and with three days to go in the 1982-83 season they still had a chance for second place. On the very last night third place slipped away from them and they found themselves facing the powerful Oilers in the playoffs. Edmonton quickly ended the Winnipeg season in three straight games.

Coach Tom Watt said he was satisfied with many aspects of the season and is confident the Jets are moving ahead at a steady pace.

"We have the youngest team in the league," added General Manager John Ferguson, "but we also have experience. There are many good years ahead for this hockey club."

Dale Hawerchuk

STRENGTHS: The Jets' Dave Babych is now among the top half-dozen league defenders, a genuine all-star. Dale Hawerchuk (40-51-91) centres for two excellent wingers, Paul McLean (32-44-76) and Brian Mullen (24-26-50). Thomas Steen was a surprise 26-goal scorer last season and he's going to get even better. Laurie Boschman, acquired from Edmonton, will help the Jets become more physical.

WEAKNESSES: The supporting cast for Babych is not intimidating so defence is a problem area. There's also a lack of depth on the forward lines. Some critics say goal tending is not strong but watch Brian Hayward put his rookie problems behind him and become a reliable performer in the nets.

THE FUTURE: By trading disgruntled Dave Christian to Washington, the Jets were able to land Bob Dollas, a top-rated junior defenceman from Laval, in the entry draft. With their first choice in the draft, the Jets selected Andrew McBain, a big, tough winger. Both players appear to be ready for NHL play. So does Jim Kyte, a huge defenceman from Cornwall drafted in '82. U.S. Olympian Mark Behrend would look good in Winnipeg colours.

VANCOUVER CANUCKS

Last season the Canucks set a club record with 303 goals scored. The defence contributed 53 of them compared to a mere 26 the season before. If the forwards, aside from the line of Darcy Rota, Stan Smyl and Thomas Gradin, had scored more often the Canucks might have finished in second place in the Smythe Division. As it turned out they finished third behind the Flames, their play-off opponents in the first round. The Flames ousted the Canucks in four games, with the Canucks appearing to have only half their players going at full speed. Injuries hurt the team last season—if the players hope to improve on last season's record they'll have to stay healthy.

STRENGTHS: The Vancouver team doesn't shy away from hard work. The Rota-Smyl-Gradin line accounted for 112 goals last season. Rota was high man with 42. Rookie Pat

Richard Brodeur

Sundstrom (whose twin brother is owned by the Rangers) scored 23 times and is highly regarded. Goal tending is solid with Richard Brodeur and John Garrett guarding the nets. And young defencemen Rick Lanz and Garth Butcher are much improved while veterans Kevin McCarthy, Lars Lindgren and Harold Snepts are reliable performers.

WEAKNESSES: There are shortcomings in several areas. The NHL pace is far too quick for several Canucks. There's a lack of size and scoring ability on the wings and there are no 50-goal shooters to make up for the non-productive wingers. As a result, when the Canucks get a lead they sometimes can't hold on to it. Last season they ignored forechecking and were undisciplined in their own zone. Coach Roger Neilson will concentrate on solving these problems—it's a big job that will take time.

THE FUTURE: The Canucks are pleased with Cam Neely, their first-round draft choice in June, a solid right winger from the Portland Winter Hawks. Tony Tanti's goal-scoring skills should be much more evident this season. Moe Lemay scored 11 goals in 44 games last season and should more than double that output this time round. Both youngsters need to improve their checking. Goalie Wendall Young has a future with the Canucks and defenceman Michel Petit shows promise.

CALGARY FLAMES

The addition of almost a dozen new faces didn't help the Flames much last season. Perhaps a few more changes will help them turn things around this year.

Average is the word to describe the Flames' play last season. Even with all the lineup changes they failed to play .500 hockey. They squeezed past Vancouver in the playoffs but were overwhelmed by the Oilers in the Smythe Division final series.

Playing in the new Saddledome should give the Flames a lift. Coach Bob Johnson insists he won't settle for a repeat of the performances he got from some of his players last season. General Manager Cliff Fletcher hastens to add, "There'll be no house cleaning. Most of the changes will come from young players who are ready to step in and grab a job."

Lanny McDonald

STRENGTHS: Two of hockey's top scorers, Kent Nilsson and Lanny McDonald, are Calgary's greatest assets. Nilsson is a 100-point man and McDonald collected 66 goals last season. Paul Reinhart is an outstanding offensive defenceman (75 points last season) while Kari Eloranta is a much-improved blueliner. Watch for Eddy Beers, former L.A. King Steve Bozek and rookie Mario Simioni to make a splash this season.

WEAKNESSES: The Flames expect more from Don Edwards in goal. There are gaps defensively and a lack of depth up front. Bob Johnson pinpoints another problem when he says, "I don't just want players who can play in the league. I want players who can *win* in the league. There's a difference, you know."

THE FUTURE: Defenceman Jamie Macoun, signed late last season out of college hockey, figures prominently in the Flames' future. So does Swedish star Haken Loob, who could be "another Mats Naslund" according to Calgary scouts. Centre Dan Quinn of Belleville was the Flames' first-round draft pick in June but he'll need development time. Aside from Simioni, watch for Allan MacInnis, Todd Hooey and Yves Courteau as future Flames.

LOS ANGELES KINGS

It must be embarrassing to finish dead last in a division in which only one team finished with a better than .500 record. Yet that's what happened to the Kings last year when they stumbled to the basement of the weak Smythe Division where all teams but the Oilers lost more games than they won. Kings' owner Jerry Buss contends that it's not management's fault. He likes his team of Manager George Maguire, Coach Don Perry and Goalie Coach Rogie Vachon.

One thing the Kings should do is stop making disastrous trades with their top draft choices. Two years ago they gave up their number-one choice to Buffalo for Richard Martin. Last season

Dave Taylor

their top two choices went to Buffalo and Montreal in other bad deals. They should have learned a lesson back in '78 when they acquired goalie Ron Grahame in return for a number-one choice, for out of that transaction the rival Bruins collected a solid defenceman in Ray Bourque.

STRENGTHS: Dionne, Taylor and Simmer are the Kings' best goal-scoring threats. Dionne can be counted on for at least one more 100-point season and Bernie Nicholls, with 28 goals as a rookie, could become a big star. Former Flame Kevin Lavallee, happy to get away from Calgary, should have a big year.

WEAKNESSES: Inexperience in goal hurts the Kings and the defence constantly needs patching. Strong, mobile defenders should be high on the Kings' priority list. Their penalty-killing has been the worst in the league.

THE FUTURE: Of the 18 rookies who played at least one game with the Kings in 1982-83, several will get more ice time this season. Former Oshawa junior Dave Gans is an excellent prospect. Look for names like Warren Holmes, Dean Kennedy, Dave Morrison, Howard Scruton and Phil Sykes to appear more regularly in the Kings' line-up.

BOSTON
BRUINS

First the good news. Boston General Manager Harry Sinden was inducted into the Hockey Hall of Fame last summer, in recognition of the job he's done keeping the Bruins up with the front runners in the NHL. The bad news (for Boston fans) is that despite their 50 wins and 110 points last season, the Bruins weren't strong enough to take the Stanley Cup.

It might have been a happier ending if so many injuries hadn't killed the Bruins' chances. The loss of Steve Kasper, Terry O'Reilly, Mike Milbury and Randy Hillier for long periods hurt the team badly. Norman Leveille's career-ending brain hemorrhage was a tragedy that affected the Bruins emotionally. The wonder of it is that they

Pete Peeters

were able to collect a league-leading point total. This season they should be right back on top again, edging closer to the Cup they last won in 1972.

STRENGTHS: Pete Peeters is the league's top goalie, although his playoff efforts last spring were spotty. A tough defence led by Ray Bourque and Milbury, with Gord Kluzak coming fast, is another plus. The team also has hockey's best two-way forward in Rick Middleton and a superb playmaker in Barry Pederson. The Crowder brothers (nicknamed Corn and Clam) and Mike Krushelnyski further bolster the team's potential for winning. Balance, depth, experience and Bruin pride will carry this team a long distance.

WEAKNESSES: Peeters' playoff performance raises the question: Is he really as good as he looked in 1982-83? With Wayne Cashman retired, who will provide the leadership? Coach Gerry Cheevers must be thankful he doesn't have much else to worry about.

THE FUTURE: Defensively, the Bruins see a bright future for last season's rookie Gord Kluzak, who sparkled in the playoffs. Other potential Bruins, players like Dave Barr, Scott McLellan, Dave Donnelly and Kevin Markwart (the Bruins' top draft choice last June), will have trouble cracking the solid Boston line-up.

BUFFALO
SABRES

The Buffalo Sabres, with seven rookies on the roster, charged into the Stanley Cup playoffs last spring and stunned the Montreal Canadiens with three straight victories, two of them on shutouts by goalie Bob Sauvé. The Sabres hoped to give the Bruins a similar shock treatment in the Adams Division finals but the Bruins withstood the charge, and led by Rick Middleton and Barry Pederson, chased the Sabres out of the Stanley Cup hunt. Now Buffalo is back—wiser, older and bolder—and expecting to pound on Lord Stanley's door come May.

Lindy Ruff

STRENGTHS: The coaching of Scotty Bowman always means a team that plays aggressively in both ends of the rink. Bowman's faith in rookie rearguards Phil Housley and Hannu Virta paid off handsomely. And the team has a dangerous trio in Dave Andreychuk, Mal Davis and Paul Cyr, plus Gilbert Perreault (30 goals) is coming off another big season. On defence, Mike Ramsay has developed into one of the league's premier players.

WEAKNESSES: Despite taking good advantage of home ice in tiny Memorial Auditorium, the Sabres have had problems winning away from home. Inexperience may still be a minor problem, but probably not for long with Bowman's coaching. Goal tending could be a trouble spot but Bob Sauvé looked sharp in the playoffs last spring and should get a majority of starts.

THE FUTURE: More kids are on the way. With three first-round choices in the entry draft, Bowman selected American ace goalie Tom Barrasso (who may be a couple of years away), sturdy winger Normand Lacombe from New Hampshire University and Adam Creighton, a big centre from the Ottawa 67s. Réal Cloutier, acquired in a trade with Quebec, should find new life in Buffalo.

MONTREAL CANADIENS

When the Buffalo Sabres quickly eliminated Montreal last April in the first round of the play-offs, a new broom swept through the Forum offices. Out went Irving Grundman and in came Serge Savard with a free hand to change the team to his liking. He quickly re-signed Coach Bob Berry and hired popular Jacques Lemaire as assistant coach. The pressure is on the rookie general manager to bring the Canadiens back to respectability. If Savard makes a couple of wrong moves his popularity may not last long.

Savard surprised a few people his first day on the job by saying, "I think Guy Lafleur is still a great player. I believe he can score 50 goals again."

Mark Napier

STRENGTHS: Pride and tradition are two of Montreal's greatest strengths, and Savard will make sure that current Canadiens don't lose sight of those qualities. Larry Robinson still does the job on defence. Pierre Mondou, Mark Napier and Mario Tremblay are dangerous with the puck and Mats Naslund puts spark into the Montreal attack. Lafleur is still a plus but not likely to score 50 goals as Savard suggests.

WEAKNESSES: Average goal tending and problems on defence hurt the Canadiens. Ric Nattress, Craig Ludwig and Bill Root have the potential to fill the gaps left by Engblom and Langway, but will they? Another good rushing defenceman would help. Lafleur no longer dominates games as he did in the past. Fans expect a little more from Steve Shutt, Bob Gainey, Ryan Walter and Doug Wickenheiser. Finally, the Montreal power play is not intimidating and the penalty killing is below par.

THE FUTURE: Savard ignited applause at the draft meetings when he selected Soviet superstar Vladislav Tretiak in the seventh round. Wouldn't it be a coup if the Soviets could be talked into letting Tretiak finish his career in the NHL? Alfie Turcotte, a centre from the Portland Winter Hawks, may need some seasoning before donning a Montreal uniform. He was Montreal's first-round choice in '83 and was MVP of the Memorial Cup Tournament. Olympian Chris Chelios has an excellent chance of fitting in on defence.

QUEBEC
NORDIQUES

The Quebec Nordiques hope that most of their
disappointments are behind them. In 1982-83
they had a disappointing season (a .500 record
which left them in fourth place in the Adams
Division) and a disappointing playoff series in the
first round against Boston, in which they were
eliminated in four games. They also had a high
rate of injuries, including a broken leg to star
defenceman Mario Marois and a shoulder injury
to superstar Marian Stastny.

At season's end Quebec management issued a
"we want a more consistent effort from our players, or else" edict and the team braced itself for
changes. Veteran André Dupont retired and veterans Marc Tardif, Réal Cloutier and Jacques Richard were told they did not figure in the future
of the Nordiques. The house cleaning in Quebec
was similar to the one in Montreal—only
Quebec's was on the ice, not in the front office.

Peter Stasny

STRENGTHS: Without Peter, Marian and Anton Stastny the Nordiques would be much closer to the bottom of the standings. But in addition to the Stastnys, Dave Hunter, Michel Goulet and Wilf Paiement can stir things up. Dan Bouchard is a proven netminder although it's debatable whether he's worth the tremendous salary he earns. Next to the Oilers, the Nordiques possess the best attack, with 343 goals last season.

WEAKNESSES: Quebec's defence is shaky. If Mario Marois makes a strong comeback the Nordiques will have at least one defenceman who knows what to do. The others are rather ordinary although young Randy Moller shows some promise. Quebec needs a strong third line to be competitive. The special teams—power play and penalty killing—are not effective.

THE FUTURE: In a last-minute trade before the June draft the Nordiques acquired Tony McKegney, Buffalo's leading scorer last season (36 goals), along with André Savard and J. F. Sauvé. All three should help the Nordiques. Yves Heroux, a big right winger with a knack for scoring goals, was drafted in the second round and may have to wait a year or two before cracking the line-up. Also eager to play are Mike Eagles, David Shaw and goalie Mario Gosselin.

HARTFORD
WHALERS

Enthusiasm is what Emile Francis is demanding of all the Hartford Whalers. (Of course, if he can find a player who lacks enthusiasm but has skills like Gretzky, Francis will take him.) Moving the Whalers up the hockey ladder is the greatest challenge Francis has faced in his long hockey career, but the new general manager comes in at the right time. The Whalers have been to the bottom and now, with some good draft choices and with Ron Francis to lead them, things are looking up in Hartford.

Ron Francis

STRENGTHS: Goalie Greg Millen was credited with 14 of the Whalers' 19 wins last season and is better than his 4.81 goals-against average indicates. In Ron Francis the Whalers possess one of the best young pros in hockey. Blaine Stoughton still scores 40 to 50 goals a year, and Mark Johnston got 31 goals last season. Risto Siltanen is an excellent defenceman and Chris Kotsopolous gets better each year.

Apart from the players the best thing the Whalers have going for them is the new general manager, who brings much-needed strength and wisdom to the front office. And new coach Jack Evans works well with young players—another reason the Whalers may move up a notch or two.

WEAKNESSES: Defence is shaky: the Whalers gave up 403 goals last year, the only club to allow that many. There's also a lack of speed and mobility in their own zone. Their power play is non-productive (only Detroit's was worse) and there's a lack of depth up front.

THE FUTURE: The Whalers surprised everybody in June by picking Sylvain Turgeon just behind number-one draft choice Brian Lawton in the entry draft. Turgeon is an outstanding skater with a scoring touch. He could fit in immediately. So could Mark Patterson, Swedish ace Ulf Samuelsson, and following the Olympics, Canadian team member Kevin Dineen.

PHILADELPHIA FLYERS

The Philadelphia Flyers enjoyed an outstanding season in 1982-83, but their performance was tarnished by a rapid exit in the first round of the playoffs against the Rangers. After winning 49 games in regular season play the Flyers were rubbed out in three straight games by the fast-skating Rangers.

During the playoffs one Philadelphia writer called the Flyers' conduct "reprehensible and panic-stricken. They played viciously and they played dumb." General Manager and Coach Bob McCammon has to take much of the blame for

Bobby Clarke

the playoff performance. He had a chance to rest some of the veteran players late in the season and refused to do so. It was also his responsibility to get his team ready for playoff action and the Flyers were simply not prepared.

STRENGTHS: The goal tending of Pelle Lindbergh and Bob Froese should be even better this season. Defenceman Mark Howe is the Flyers' best player and possibly the best defenceman in hockey, and Brian Propp (40 goals) and Ron Flockhart (29 goals) are proven scorers. Finally, the leadership of oldtimers like Bobby Clarke and Darryl Sittler can't be underrated.

WEAKNESSES: Aside from Howe there are no standouts on defence. More speed is needed on the blueline and the Flyers' power play needs revamping. It was 15th in the league last season. There is also concern about lack of determination on the part of the Flyers, in light of how they folded to the Rangers last spring.

THE FUTURE: Ron Sutter, the Flyers' number-one draft choice in '82, is ready for NHL play. Two fast centres from Maine, Len Hackborn and Steve Tsijura, rate attention although Tsijura is small. The Flyers traded their first-round draft choice in 1983. Their second choice, Peter Zezel, is a year or two away. Rick Gal, a former Lethbridge star, and defenceman André Villeneuve are future Flyers.

NEW YORK ISLANDERS

The Islanders looked as if they were playing possum last season, strolling through the regular season as if winning didn't matter much anymore. They won 12 fewer games than the year before and finished with 22 fewer points, and by midseason the alarm bells were ringing throughout the Nassau County Coliseum. But when coach Al Arbour barked "It's playoff time" the Isles snapped to attention. They defeated the determined Capitals, the speedy Rangers and the rugged Bruins before clashing with the Oilers for the Stanley Cup. Superb goal tending by Billy Smith, a relentless attack and strong defensive play carried the Isles to their fourth straight Cup.

During the finals the Islanders astonished everyone with their four-game sweep of Wayne Gretzky's gang, and even held Gretzky off the scoresheet in the series. Billy Smith sparkled in goal and won the Conn Smythe Trophy for his play. The Islanders need one more Cup to tie the Montreal Canadiens' five-straight record set from 1956 to 1960.

Mike Bossy

STRENGTHS: The Islanders' defence, anchored by all-star Denis Potvin, makes opposing forwards earn every scrap of ice. Mike Bossy's scoring (three straight 60-goal seasons), the brilliance of Bryan Trottier and a supporting cast that includes Clark Gillies, John Tonelli, Bob Bourne, Bob Nystrom and Brent and Duane Sutter makes Islander-bashing a major accomplishment for rival NHL clubs. Bill Torrey, considered by some to be the league's best general manager, will do a little fine tuning for the 1983-84 season to keep the Islanders at or near the top.

WEAKNESSES: Last season the Islanders appeared to rest on their laurels much of the season, and didn't really pull themselves together until the playoffs. Al Arbour will have to watch out for a day when he yells, "Wake up, guys, it's playoff time!" and nobody's listening.

THE FUTURE: Sooner or later the Islanders must find a place for goalie Kelly Hrudey, whose minor league stats are impressive. Drafting third in the entry draft, the Isles grabbed Pat LaFontaine (235 points last season with Verdun juniors) but few 18-year-olds get to play with the defending champions. Other young stars looking for positions include Neil Coulter, Paul Boutillier, Greg Gilbert, Gord Dineen, Dave Simpson and defenceman Gerald Diduck of Lethbridge, another first-round choice in June. After the Olympics, look for Canadian team member Pat Flatley to join the Isles.

WASHINGTON
CAPITALS

Now that the Washington Capitals have proven they can play with the best teams in the Patrick Division, they want to displace some of those clubs and move to the front of the class. General Manager David Poile says, "Last year we were thinking of fourth place and making the playoffs for the first time. Now we're ready to move right to the front of our division and stay there all season long."

It's unfortunate the Capitals had to face the powerful Islanders in their first-round playoff match last spring. Washington's playoff inexperience showed and they bowed out in four games. On an individual player basis, the Islanders totalled 1339 playoff games to the Caps' 253.

In 1982-83 Washington finished the regular season with 94 points, their best record in the short history of the team.

Rod Langway

STRENGTHS: A strong defence led by Rod Langway and Brian Engblom, along with Scott Stevens, is moving up fast into the front rank of the league's defenders. The Caps have a good mix up front with Mike Gartner (38 goals) and Bobby Carpenter (32 goals) putting punch into the attack. Strong defensive forwards and good penalty killing are also part of the team's strength, plus the added confidence that comes from making the playoffs for the first time. A good coach in Bryan Murray and a shrewd general manager in David Poile will also help the team's chances in 1983-84.

WEAKNESSES: The team has problems in a poor power play and inconsistent goal tending. Both Pat Riggin and Al Jensen blow hot and cold. And finally, there's still a need for more depth.

THE FUTURE: Dave Christian, happy to be away from Winnipeg, should be a plus for the Caps. They can't count on any immediate help from the '83 draft since they traded their top two choices to Winnipeg (Bob Dollas) and Montreal (Todd Francis), but Dean Evanson, Mike Siltala and goalie Peter Sidorkiewicz are excellent prospects.

NEW YORK RANGERS

The Rangers came on with a rush last season and their momentum carried them right past the stunned Philadelphia Flyers in the Patrick Division semi-finals. The Rangers managed to out-hustle and outskate the Flyers and were not stopped until they ran into a poised New York Islander team in the Division finals.

After the final game with the Isles, Ranger General Manager Craig Patrick grimaced and said, "Well, back to the drawing board." A few days later Patrick traded popular stars Ron Duguay, Eddio Mio and Ed Johnstone to Detroit for huge defenceman Willie Huber and forwards Mike Blaisdell and Mark Osborne.

Barry Beck

STRENGTHS: One of the Rangers' greatest strengths is breakneck speed. Coach Herb Brooks has spent two seasons stressing flow and motion with his players, and when the combination clicks other teams find them difficult to stop. Other assets are Mike Rogers and Mark Pavelich, both small but elusive and dangerous around the net. Don Maloney is another good goal scorer. On defence, big Barry Beck keeps things tidy in his own zone and Routsalainen is an excellent offensive defenceman.

WEAKNESSES: Can injuries be called a weakness? The Rangers always seem to be hit harder than other clubs in the injury department, possibly because some of the players are so small. Look for Coach Brooks to beef up a couple of his forward lines.

The Rangers' goal tending has been inconsistent in the past and that could be a problem area with Mio gone. Also, after Beck and Routsalainen the team's defence is not outstanding.

THE FUTURE: The Rangers can't wait for the Olympics to be over. That's when they hope to get outstanding defenceman James Patrick in their line-up. He bears a "can't miss" label. Chris Kontos, a first-round draft choice in 1982, played 44 games with the Rangers last season and may be ready for regular work. College goalie Ron Scott, for whom the Rangers paid a bundle, figures prominently in their future.

NEW JERSEY
DEVILS

Kansas City, Colorado, the Meadowlands in New Jersey—that's the route the Devils (formerly the Scouts and the Rockies) have followed in their quest for big-league acceptance. Now that they've found a home and enough fans to support them they'd better concentrate on coming up with a hockey team. Last season's record of 17 victories, the fewest in the league, is the tipoff that plenty of changes are needed in the Devils' camp.

"We want lots of young people to take over," says General Manager Bill MacMillan. "If half a dozen new kids are ready to step in, we'll welcome them."

Chico Resch

STRENGTHS: Chico Resch, who played in 68 games last year, is one of the most reliable goalies in hockey, and the Devils have steady Ron Low as backup. Aaron Broten is a clever young playmaker and Don Lever a diligent worker who'll score 25 to 30 goals. Jeff Larmer's quick hands should lead to plenty of goals too. Paul Gagné had a strong second half last season. Veterans Mel Bridgman and Phil Russell, acquired in a trade with Calgary, bring experience and muscle to the Devils.

WEAKNESSES: The New Jersey defence is porous. Bob Lorimer and Mike Kitchen work hard but opposing forwards invade the Devils' zone with ease. Because young players can make plenty of mistakes, reliance on kids like Joe Cirella, Pat Verbeek, Ken Daneyko, Rich Chernomaz and Bryan Trottier's kid brother Rocky may result in another long, unproductive season for the Devils.

THE FUTURE: Looks bright if the young players mature quickly. Watch for former Oshawa star right winger John McLean to make a good impression. He was the Devils' first choice (number six overall) in the entry draft. Pat Verbeek played in six games last season and made a strong impression.

PITTSBURGH PENGUINS

When a team wins only 18 games and gives up almost 400 goals it's obvious that roster changes must follow. The Penguins, who finished dead last in 1982-83, face a dismal future and have nowhere to turn for help. The best player on their Baltimore farm team last season was Mitch Lamoureaux, who scored a record 57 goals and added 50 assists. The trouble is that Lamoureaux is small and lacks takeoff speed. The Pens would have had first choice in June's entry draft if they hadn't traded that choice to Minnesota last season in the swap of George Ferguson for Anders Hakansson and Ron Meighan. So long, Brian Lawton.

Randy Carlyle

STRENGTHS: Doug Shedden and Mike Bullard are two young forwards with offensive skills, and Randy Carlyle, a former Norris Trophy winner, is a key man on defence. Goal tender Michel Dion played some strong games despite the bombardment he faced. Pittsburgh has an excellent power play scorer in Paul Gardner.

WEAKNESSES: Backup goalie Denis Herron gave up over five goals a game last season. The specialty teams were weak and Pittsburgh's power play, once one of the league's best, was non-existent for long stretches. The penalty killing was dreadful: the Pens gave up 110 goals while playing short-handed, the only team to allow more than 100. I think five or six of last year's Penguins should have been playing in the minors. General Manager and Coach Eddie Johnston hopes the NHL experience they gained will serve them well this season.

THE FUTURE: Despite his lack of size, Mitch Lamoureaux may push his way on to the Pens. Goalie Roberto Romano had an excellent year with Baltimore. Ron Meighan, since coming over from Minnesota, has blossomed. Todd Charlesworth, a defenceman from Oshawa and the Pens' second-round draft choice in June, has an outside chance of sticking. Rich Sutter may be the best of the rookies.

HOW THEY'LL FINISH

It's always fun to predict next season's order of finish of the 21 NHL teams. I'll make my choices on one side of the page. You make yours on the other. At the end of the season we can check back and see how accurate we were.

Brian McFarlane _____

(Your name here)

Norris Division

Chicago	_____
Minnesota	_____
Toronto	_____
St. Louis	_____
Detroit	_____

Smythe Division

Edmonton	_____
Winnipeg	_____
Vancouver	_____
Calgary	_____
Los Angeles	_____

Wayne Gretzky

Adams Division

Boston   _____
Buffalo   _____
Montreal   _____
Quebec   _____
Hartford   _____

Patrick Division

Philadelphia   _____
N.Y. Islanders   _____
Washington   _____
N.Y. Rangers   _____
New Jersey   _____
Pittsburgh   _____

PICKING AN ALL-STAR TEAM

It's fun to sit down with some friends and select an all-star team. As soon as you start making your choices the arguments begin. Is Bossy better than McDonald? How can you ignore Mark Howe on defence? Who's the best left winger?

A group of us decided to select our all-star teams one night following the televising of a game.

Frank Orr, hockey writer with the *Toronto Star,* said, "I'm going to put Rick Middleton on left wing on my team."

"But you can't do that, Frank," someone objected. "Middleton's a right winger."

"I know, but he can play anywhere," was Orr's answer. "Besides, that'll give me a chance to make a line of Gretzky, Middleton and Bossy."

Doug Beeforth, producer with *Hockey Night in Canada,* liked Orr's idea so much he made a left winger of Middleton too. Don Cherry was the only one to select Larry Robinson on defence and Al Secord on left wing. When Cherry coached the Bruins Secord was one of his favourites.

I couldn't decide between Bossy and Lanny McDonald on right wing and finally opted for Bossy. He scores 50 goals or more *every* season.

All of us had trouble picking defencemen—
there are so many good ones in hockey today.
Paul Coffey of the Oilers was the only unanimous
choice, while Norris Trophy winner Rod Langway
was ignored by all but one of the selectors.

The selectors included hockey announcers
Danny Gallivan, Gilles Tremblay and Don
Cherry of *Hockey Night in Canada,* Dan Kelly
and Gary Green of the USA TV Network, sports-
writer Frank Orr of the *Toronto Star,* Doug Beeforth, producer of *Hockey Night in Canada* and
myself. Here are our choices:

Brian McFarlane
Hockey Night in Canada

Goalie:	Pete Peeters
Defence:	Paul Coffey
Defence:	Ray Bourque
Centre:	Wayne Gretzky
Rt. Wing:	Mike Bossy
Left Wing:	Mark Messier

Danny Gallivan
Hockey Night in Canada

Goalie:	Pete Peeters
Defence:	Paul Coffey
Defence:	Denis Potvin
Centre:	Wayne Gretzky
Rt. Wing:	Rick Middleton
Left Wing:	Mark Messier

Don Cherry
Hockey Night in Canada

Goalie:	Pete Peeters
Defence:	Larry Robinson
Defence:	Denis Potvin
Centre:	Wayne Gretzky
Rt. Wing:	Rick Middleton
Left Wing:	Al Secord

Gilles Tremblay
Hockey Night in Canada

Goalie:	Pete Peeters
Defence:	Paul Coffey
Defence:	Ray Bourque
Centre:	Wayne Gretzky
Rt. Wing:	Mike Bossy
Left Wing:	Mark Messier

Dan Kelly
USA Network

Goalie:	Pete Peeters
Defence:	Paul Coffey
Defence:	Rod Langway
Centre:	Wayne Gretzky
Rt. Wing:	Mike Bossy
Left Wing:	Mark Messier

Gary Green
USA Network

Goalie:	Pete Peeters
Defence:	Paul Coffey
Defence:	Doug Wilson
Centre:	Wayne Gretzky
Rt. Wing:	Mike Bossy
Left Wing:	Mark Messier

Frank Orr
Toronto Star

Goalie:	Pete Peeters
Defence:	Denis Potvin
Defence:	Paul Coffey
Centre:	Wayne Gretzky
Rt. Wing:	Mike Bossy
Left Wing:	Rick Middleton

Doug Beeforth,
Producer
Hockey Night in Canada

Goalie:	Pete Peeters
Defence:	Denis Potvin
Defence:	Doug Wilson
Centre:	Wayne Gretzky
Rt. Wing:	Mike Bossy
Left Wing:	Rick Middleton

Now it's your turn. Fill in the names of your own hockey all-star team.

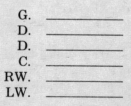

G. _____
D. _____
D. _____
C. _____
RW. _____
LW. _____

I REMEMBER A KID NAMED GRETZKY

Ten years ago I played a hockey game with the NHL Oldtimers in Hamilton, Ontario. Our opposition that night was a team called the No Stars, a traditional team name for media types—people who work for newspapers and radio stations.

In the warm-up before the game I noticed a little fellow skating around the ice with blond hair puffing out from under his helmet. Surely *he* wasn't going to play against us! He was dwarfed by the mass of bodies warming up around him. I thought perhaps he was the son of one of the players on the other team, or even the team mascot.

But no! When the game started there he was at centre ice, ready to face off.

I said to our coach, "Who's the little kid at centre?"

"Oh, the other team pulled him in from Brantford for the game," he said. "He's supposed to be the best young player for his age in this area. Name's Gretzky."

Gretzky! I'd heard of Gretzky. I'd read all about him after he'd been the best player in the big International Pee Wee tournament in Quebec

City earlier that season. He'd drawn the same sort of rave reviews that Guy Lafleur and Gilbert Perreault had received when they were hot-shot pee wees in Quebec.

I'd read about the unusual white hockey gloves he wore and how he had the big number nine on his back. At Quebec he was the most talked-about, most-interviewed, most-photographed young player in the tournament. When he skated around the arena fans would nudge each other and say "C'est le grand Gretzky...there's the Great Gretzky."

In one game in Quebec, Wayne scored seven goals and added four assists. Later his father asked him why he didn't score eight goals—he could have but he passed the puck to a teammate instead—to break the tournament record held by Guy Lafleur. Wayne just shrugged and said, "Gee, Dad, I didn't even think about the record."

Playing against Wayne Gretzky that night in Hamilton, I could easily spot his potential. He was a fine skater and very clever with the puck. He scored a couple of goals against us and might have scored more if he'd had the help of wingers who weren't awkward and overweight.

After the game I talked to Wayne, his parents and his coach, Ron St. Amand. Ron told me Wayne had already scored 1000 goals in minor hockey, a staggering total.

"Fortunately," said Ron, "Wayne is able to take all the attention he gets in stride. If I thought, or his parents thought, he'd get a swelled head over all the publicity, then we'd cool him off pretty quick. But we've never even had to discuss it. He's just a normal young guy who happens to have great natural talent. His only fear is that he might not grow big enough to play pro hockey."

From that night on I've followed Wayne's career with keen interest. A year or two later he moved to Toronto to play Junior B hockey. At 16 he was drafted by Sault Ste. Marie, a Junior A team. When he reached the Soo he was disappointed to find his favorite number nine was

being worn by another player. The coach said, "Wayne, why not take another number and make it uniquely yours? How about wearing 99?" Wayne thought that was a terrific idea.

Wayne scored 70 goals in 64 games as a junior and was soon lured away from amateur hockey by the World Hockey Association. Nelson Skalbania, owner of the Indianapolis team, signed him to a staggering contract for a 17-year-old—$875,000 to be paid over four years.

But Skalbania ran into financial problems and sold Wayne's contract to another millionaire, Peter Pocklington, owner of the WHA Edmonton Oilers. On Wayne's eighteenth birthday Pocklington tore up his old contract and gave him a better one, a 21-year personal services contract worth a staggering five million dollars... plus a new Lincoln Continental every year.

Endorsements fell his way, so many of them that their dollar value almost matched his hockey income. His agent, Gus Badali, would kid him and say, "Wayne, hurry up and start shaving so we can get you an aftershave endorsement."

Wayne scored 110 points in his rookie (and only) season in the WHA. When Edmonton joined the NHL the following year he scored 137 points and left no doubts that he had arrived as a superstar. He scored 164 points in his second NHL season and was simply unstoppable in his third. No one in hockey thought it possible but Gretzky did it: 92 goals and 120 assists for 212 points in 80 games.

Bobby Orr, one of the world's great players,

watched Gretzky play and said, "If Wayne is influencing the millions of kids I think he is—thank God he's around."

Phil Esposito, another hockey great, recalled a phone conversation with his father, who was part owner of the junior team in Sault Ste. Marie. "Yeah, he called one night to say he'd just seen a sixteen-year-old kid who was going to break all my scoring records. He said his name was Gretzky and was just as good as Orr. My dad always did know talent when he saw it."

Last season Gretzky saw much less ice time than the year before and still managed 196 points, including 71 goals. In three NHL seasons The Kid has scored more goals (269) and more points (511) than many scoring stars who are honoured in the Hall of Fame after careers spanning 10 and 15 years.

Today a Gretzky autograph is a hockey fan's most coveted possession. Wayne says he doesn't mind the autograph hunters. He remembers his mother chasing around after Bobby Hull to get an autograph for him when he was just starting out in hockey. "I remember how meaningful it was to me."

He laughs when people say he's a complete hockey player. "I'm still trying to improve every part of my game," he says. "When I first came up, my shot would hardly break a pane of glass. I've got to keep working at it."

If he still worries about his shot there's one thing that no longer bothers him . . . and that's never growing big enough to play NHL hockey.

BUFFALO'S HOPES HINGE ON HOUSLEY

A few years ago I was in Minnesota for a hockey telecast featuring a game between the Toronto Maple Leafs and the North Stars.

In the lobby of the hotel I ran into a couple of hockey scouts heading out for a high school game nearby.

"Looking for another Neal Broten?" I asked. Broten had been Minnesota's most-publicized high school player.

"Yeah, and there's one out there," was the answer. "A young player named Housley we want to look at."

Off they went and I all but forgot the name Housley until the June draft meetings in Montreal in 1982. "The Buffalo Sabres draft Phil Housley," announced Scotty Bowman, the Sabres' General Manager.

Eyebrows shot up. Bowman had taken an 18-year-old from South St. Paul high school in Minnesota as the Sabres' number-one choice and the sixth player drafted overall. The only U.S. high school player chosen higher in the draft was Bobby Carpenter, taken third by Washington in 1981.

Phil Housley

Earlier, Bowman had dropped hints that he'd seen a young player with exceptional skills, a boy he hoped would still be available in the entry draft. After Housley became a Sabre he drew high praise from Bowman, who said Housley reminded him of Bobby Orr in the way he performed.

Assistant Coach Jim Roberts added, "From the first time we saw him take the ice in training camp, we knew he was something special."

Playing in the NHL meant a departure from Housley's personal game plan. He had intended to go to college and hoped to play for the U.S. team in the 1984 Olympics, defending the title won at Lake Placid in 1980.

"Being drafted in the first round forced me to think seriously about pro hockey," Housley says. "I was glad it was the Sabres who took me because I'd been told they were going to give their young players a lot of ice time.

"I'll still get my college education, I hope. I'll go to summer school each year until I get my degree."

Housley is that rare breed of player who feels at home at centre ice as well as on defence. Like Orr, he has the knack of doing the right thing at the right time as well as anticipating what others are going to do. It's a gift all great players have.

LARMER WINS
THE CALDER

Every season a handful of rookie players prove they're not only ready to play in the NHL, they're ready to star in the NHL. Last season was no exception as a surprising number of first-year players impressed their coaches, their teammates and the fans: Phil Housley and Hannu Virta in Buffalo, Brian Bellows in Minnesota, Mats Naslund and Guy Carbonneau in Montreal, Brian Mullen in Winnipeg, Dan Daoust, Peter Ihnacak and Walt Poddubny in Toronto, Bernie Nicholls in Los Angeles, Steve Larmer in Chicago, Mike Krushelnyski and Gord Kluzak in Boston, Pelle Lindbergh and Bob Froese (both goalies) in Philadelphia, and many, many more.

Prior to last season, if you'd been asked to predict a Calder Trophy winner for the rookie of the year you probably would have chosen Gord Kluzak, Brian Bellows or Gary Nyland. After all, in the 1982 June draft Kluzak was chosen number one, Bellows number two and Nyland number three.

But Kluzak saw little ice time with Boston until the final few weeks of the season. Bellows, who's a hard worker but not a flashy player, didn't find his stride until the second half, and Nyland was injured in training camp and missed most of the season. He's eligible for the rookie award again this year.

Steve Larmer

Few would have predicted a rookie race between Phil Housley, an 18-year-old defenceman fresh out of high school in Minnesota, and Steve Larmer of Chicago, who almost didn't make the team in training camp. But at season's end they were the two finalists in the voting.

In June, at the annual NHL Congress in Montreal, the coveted Calder trophy went to Steve Larmer.

Larmer, whose brother Jeff was a rookie with the New Jersey Devils, joined the Hawks after a year in the American Hockey League with New Brunswick. Orval Tessier, the new Chicago coach, had also been Larmer's coach in the American League. Tessier knew what Larmer could do and how hard he worked, so he placed him on a line with Denis Savard and Al Secord. The line soon became one of the most feared in hockey. Savard collected 120 points while Larmer checked in with 90, including 43 goals.

Larmer was a big factor in Chicago's rise to the top of the Norris Division. It was puzzling why he was still available in the entry draft of 1981 after 119 other amateurs had been selected. He was a sixth-round choice.

Housley on the other hand, was regarded as the best high school player in the United States when Buffalo made him their number-one choice (sixth overall) in 1982.

Like Bobby Orr, to whom he has been compared, Housley displayed great offensive ability, scoring 19 goals and 47 assists to finish the season tied for third in rookie scoring with Peter Ihnacak.

BATTLING BILLY SMITH

Soon after the New York Islanders won their fourth straight Stanley Cup last May there were reports that goalie Billy Smith would be traded. It was said that the Isles would swap Smith, the only player left from the team that joined the NHL in 1972, so that two young goalies, Roland Melanson and Kelly Hrudey, would get more ice time.

What did Smith think of the trade rumours? "I know they're not going to trade me," he said on the day he picked up a new Pontiac Trans Am from *Sport* Magazine as MVP of the playoffs. "You don't win four Stanley Cups and end up by trading a guy. That's foolishness.

"If the Islanders lost the Cup next year, fans would jump all over management and say 'You had a guy who won the Cup four years in a row and you dump him?' No, there's nothing to it. I'd like to win the Cup every year for another four or five years and then I'll retire. After that, they can't blame me if we lose it."

There are many players, coaches and fans who look forward to the retirement of Battling Billy. The aggressive streak he displays often infuriates opponents.

Edmonton Oiler Coach Glen Sather says, "Smith plays like a maniac. He swings the stick around like a hatchet."

Billy Smith

In the Stanley Cup finals, after Smith dropped Wayne Gretzky and Glenn Anderson with his flailing goalstick, the *Edmonton Journal* identified him as *PUBLIC ENEMY NO. 1.* In the accompanying story there were references to Smith as "Mr. Obnoxious," "Jack the Ripper" and "a creep."

After the Islanders demolished the Oilers in four straight games, Smith didn't hide his bitter feelings about his opponents.

"I had no trouble getting up for any of the games with the Oilers in the final series," he said. "Because of all the abuse I took, I just wanted to give it to them. I was at the rink earlier than I've ever been, just wanting to get out there and play. I hated the Oilers so much, I just couldn't think about losing."

Smith also admitted taking a dive in the final game to help the Islander cause. When Glenn Anderson slashed him in the third period Smith fell to the ice, apparently injured. As soon as the referee gave Anderson a five-minute penalty, Smith jumped up and resumed his place in goal.

He said later, "All I did was what Gretzky did in the second game of the series. He lay down and cried and did everything else to get a major penalty called on me. I just showed him that two can play at that game.

"I think Wayne is a perfect gentleman and a great spokesman for the NHL off the ice," says Smith. "But he's the biggest crybaby ever on the ice. Wayne doesn't come back into his own end, either. One day I'm going to take him by the hand and introduce him to his goalie."

Over the years, the outspoken Smith has been one of the most dependable guys around in clutch situations. His playoff record stands at 68-22, including a remarkable 17-1 in last season's march to the Stanley Cup.

Several years ago when the Islanders alternated goalies in the playoffs, neither Smith nor Chico Resch sparkled, so the Islanders decided to go with one man and traded Resch. It was an unpopular decision because Resch was loved by the fans and the media. But the results have been satisfying. Smith, who is physically stronger than Resch, has tremendous concentration and can close out everything around him.

He did it again so well last spring that he was awarded the Conn Smythe Trophy as the most valuable player in the playoffs. One of his rewards was meeting President Ronald Reagan at the White House. He promptly presented the President with a new goalstick and suggested he use it to keep Congress in line.

MARK MESSIER'S GROWING PAINS

Young hockey stars are the envy of every kid in Canada. The good ones jump from junior hockey to the NHL, where they sign million-dollar contracts and a million autographs. It's a glamorous life of goals, fancy clothes and fantastic cars.

Mark Messier is one of the good ones. Like Wayne Gretzky, he's young (eight days older than Wayne), he's talented and he's an Edmonton Oiler. For months he's witnessed the staggering amount of attention lavished on Gretzky. If he's envious, it doesn't show.

"Wayne deserves everything he gets," says Mark. "All the publicity, all the money he makes, whatever he gets, he's earned. Don't forget, a lot of responsibility goes along with his fame. He doesn't have his summers to himself. He has all those endorsements and all that travel. It's a good thing he's very mature. He matured faster than most of us on the team. Maybe he had to."

Messier himself jumped from junior hockey at age 17 where he earned seven dollars a game (if his team won, less if they lost) to over $100,000 a year with Cincinnati of the WHA. "If I was slow to live up to my potential it was my own fault,"

Mark Messier

admits Mark. "It was a pretty fast life when I broke in. There were lots of things to see and do and I just didn't concentrate on hockey enough."

Coach Glen Sather of the Oilers understands Mark's growing pains. "I've seen it all before," says Sather. "Most teenagers who get a potful of money, a new car, some new clothes and have no parents around to lay down the law are going to get into a little trouble. Hockey players may take a little longer to mature because most of their decisions are made for them . . . like when to play and practise, when to catch a plane, when to eat."

Sather hasn't always shown such tolerance. In Messier's first season, after he missed a plane and was late for a bus, he was quickly shipped off to the Central League, where he had plenty of time to mull over his mistakes.

"I decided right then, when I got a second chance I'd bust my butt so I'd never have to go back to the minors," says Mark.

What a difference his change in attitude made. In Mark's first two NHL seasons he scored a mere 35 goals. With his new-found perspective he zoomed to 50 goals in his third year and 48 last season.

But he's still not too serious for a little fun. When a reporter caught him munching on a grilled cheese sandwich and wolfing down some ketchup-soaked french fries before last year's all-star game, Messier grinned and said, "Hey, this is what Gretzky eats before a game. Maybe this is the secret to playing just like him."

FEARLESS MARK HOWE

There's an inner fear among hockey players, a fear that is seldom discussed. But it's there. It's the fear of a career-ending injury. A broken leg, a back injury, a stick in the eye are hockey hazards that may be just over the next blueline or in the next melee in the crease.

Hockey is for the healthy. Ask Bobby Orr, whose crippled knees prematurely ended his career. Ask Greg Neeld, a brilliant junior star who lost an eye to a hockey stick and never got a chance to play.

Ask Mark Howe of the Philadelphia Flyers, runner-up to Rod Langway as best defenceman in hockey last season. Howe was lucky; the injury he suffered only came close to ending his career. Howe figured less than half a centimetre made the difference for him between skating again and being paralyzed for life.

It happened in 1980 when Howe was a star defenceman for the Hartford Whalers. He was checked by the Islanders' John Tonelli in front of the goal. The goal stanchion became unhinged as Howe flew into the net and the sharp, spear-like metal section at the base of the goal pierced Howe's buttocks. He was out of action for weeks and only last season, after the Whalers traded him to Philadelphia, did he finally regain his strength.

Mark Howe

Before the accident there were many who felt that Howe was hockey's top defenceman. In the 1980 ballotting for the all-star team, he'd out-pointed veterans like Larry Robinson and Borje Salming. After the injury there were fears that he'd never return to his former level.

The Philadelphia Flyers were willing to gamble that he would. They arranged a complicated trade. Ken Linesman, Greg Adams and the Flyers' first draft choice in 1983 went to Hartford for Howe.

In Howe, a 27-year-old veteran of nine pro seasons in the NHL and the WHA, the Flyers got a lot more than they bargained for. Back at full strength, Howe anchored the Flyers' defence. He was brilliant in his own zone and when he spotted an opening he amazed the Flyer fans with his rushes and playmaking.

"We gave up a lot to get him," said General Manager Keith Allen. "Ken Linesman, when his head is on straight, is a great little player and Greg Adams has a future in Hartford. But Howe is fantastic, the best defenceman in the game today."

Howe's surge to the forefront of NHL defencemen shouldn't surprise anyone. He's been making hockey headlines one way or another since he was 14. At that age he was a member of the Detroit Junior Red Wings, the U.S. junior champions. At 16 he played for the U.S. Olympic team at Sapporo in Japan. At 17 he was a member of the Toronto Marlboros, the Memorial Cup champions.

A year later he was starring in the WHA alongside his famous father Gordie Howe and his brother Marty. It was a story for *Believe It Or Not*—a father and two sons playing professional hockey on the same team.

When the WHA folded, Mark made the adjustment to the NHL Hartford Whalers without any problems. In his first year against the best in the NHL he collected 80 points. The closest defenceman to him in scoring was Larry Robinson of Montreal with 75.

Ranger goalie Steve Baker spoke for all goalies when he said, "Mark has one of the best shots from the point I've ever seen."

While he's pleased to be named one of the League's best defencemen, Howe won't be truly happy until he's able to celebrate a Stanley Cup victory. As his father has told him so many times, "There's no feeling quite like it."

ANOTHER LITTLE MAN MAKES IT BIG

There's a good player in the NHL who has made it big without ever winning much media attention. His name is Mike Rogers, the scoring leader of the New York Rangers. When Mike grabs the puck and flashes down the ice with it, there aren't many players who can do it better.

The trouble is, Rogers is constantly having to prove that he belongs, even though for three straight seasons—two with Hartford and one with New York—he topped 100 points.

"I've been trying to prove to people for a long, long time I can play this game," says Mike, who is now 29. "I was always small and I was never a fighter so I always concentrated on the skills of the game."

In junior hockey, as the top scorer of the Calgary Centennials, he was told to 'prove it.' Later, as an all-star in the WHA, first with Edmonton and then with the New England Whalers, he was told again to 'prove it.' Now, as a proven scoring leader in the NHL, he's not asked to 'prove it' anymore.

The Vancouver Canucks are the team most embarrassed by Roger's success. When the Whalers joined the NHL prior to the 1979-80 season the Canucks owned his rights. But they shrugged and showed no interest in the slight centreman.

Mike Rogers

Harry Neale, the man blamed for not grabbing Rogers for the Canucks when he had the opportunity, now says, "There's no question about it. I look like a fool when it comes to judging talent, all because of Mike. I'll be the first to admit it. Mike will go down in history as one of Harry Neale's biggest mistakes."

"It seems I'll never be known as a good hockey player," says Rogers. "I'll always be known as a good *small* hockey player. If I were a coach I'd like a big player with the skills of a smaller man. But as long as you're doing the job, I don't think it matters if you're 6-foot-5 or 5-foot-6."

After his first 100-point season in the NHL, Rogers said, "One year doesn't mean a thing. I'm determined to prove it wasn't just a one-shot deal." After a third straight 100-point year it appears there's little left to prove.

ALL ABOUT THE STANLEY CUP

The Stanley Cup has a fascinating history, dating back almost a century. Today's fans don't know how lucky they are even to *have* a Stanley Cup, the way the old trophy has been treated over the years. Players have lost it and stolen it. It's been kicked around and kidnapped. Enough champagne has been drunk from it to flood the Montreal Forum and enough tears shed over losing it to float a battleship.

HOCKEY'S FIRST HOLE IN ONE

One year in a Stanley Cup game the puck went skidding across the ice, then fell through a hole and disappeared. (It was many years ago and ice conditions were unpredictable in those days.) When the players finally fished the puck out the game continued. In the unofficial Stanley Cup records the game is remembered as marking hockey's first hole in one!

THE DAWSON CITY DAREDEVILS

They were daredevils all right. Can you imagine a team from Dawson City in the Yukon challenging Canada's best for the Stanley Cup? It happened in 1905 when Ottawa boasted the best hockey team in the world, the famed Ottawa Silver Seven.

Guy Lafleur

With the backing of a rich prospector, those kids from the Klondike travelled 7000 kilometres, part of the way by dog-sled, to take part in a Stanley Cup playoff series. It took them several weeks to get to Ottawa, where they were promptly walloped 9-2 in the first game of a two-game series. After the first game one of the Dawson City boys was asked his opinion of Ottawa's scoring star, Frank McGee. "Oh, he's not so hot," was the reply.

McGee showed them a thing or two in the second game. He scored a record 14 goals in one game as Ottawa triumphed 23-2. It's a record that stands to this day.

GUY LAFLEUR KIDNAPS THE CUP

Would you believe that Guy Lafleur of the Canadiens once kidnapped the Stanley Cup? After the 1979 playoffs, won by Montreal, he confessed to me at a sports banquet that he'd taken the Stanley Cup home to Thurso, Quebec to show it to all his friends and neighbours. The trouble was, he neglected to tell anyone he was borrowing the Cup and back in Montreal several officials were frantically looking for it.

Meanwhile, Guy had placed the Cup on the front lawn of his parents' home and all the fans from the area came to look at the famous trophy. But later when Guy looked out the window he saw his son, Martin, playing the garden hose on the trophy, so he hurried out to rescue the Cup and return it to Montreal as quickly as possible.

MEL HILL BECOMES A SURPRISE HERO

The name Mel Hill doesn't mean much to you, I'll bet. He wasn't much of a star even when he played for the Boston Bruins back in 1938-39. In fact, he had been cut from the New York Rangers earlier and was surprised when the Bruins picked him up.

Then, in the playoffs against his former team, the Rangers, Hill did something truly remarkable. He scored three overtime goals, including the clincher in the seventh and deciding game. From then on, and even today when oldtimers talk about Hill's performance, they call him "Sudden Death" Hill.

THE NIGHT THE ROCKET EXPLODED

Rocket Richard retired from the Montreal Canadiens in 1960 but he is still rated the greatest playoff scorer of all time. Playing against Toronto one night in 1949, Richard exploded for all five goals as the Canadiens triumphed 5-1. And after the game when the three stars were announced, Richard was named Star No. 1, Star No. 2 and Star No. 3—a hockey first. During his career, Richard scored 82 playoff goals, including six game-winners in overtime.

THE CHICAGO CAPER

In 1962 an unusual bid for the Cup was made in Chicago. In the middle of a playoff game between Montreal and Chicago (with the Canadiens losing) a fan left his seat, strolled into the lobby of the arena and cracked open the glass showcase in which the Stanley Cup was displayed. Then he hoisted the trophy over his shoulder and was walking out of the arena when some startled ushers and security men rushed after him.

"Where are you going with the Stanley Cup?" they yelled.

"Why, I'm taking it back to Montreal where it belongs," he answered.

They grabbed him and said, "You can tell it to the judge in the morning."

AIMING AT ORR

Even though Bobby Orr hasn't played an NHL game in five years, his scoring records still survive. How much longer they survive will depend on the efforts of several splendid young defencemen playing today, as well as a couple of veterans who are closing in on some of Orr's impressive marks.

Orr's record: 46 goals in a single season
It's safe. Paul Coffey of Edmonton scored 29 goals last season to lead all defencemen in goals scored. The season before, Doug Wilson of Chicago took a run at the record and finished with 39 goals.

Orr's record: 139 points in a single season
Also looks safe. Coffey was the League's leading point collector last season with 96, still a long way from Orr's total. In 1978-79, Denis Potvin came closest to the record with a 101-point season.

Orr's record: 915 career points
Brad Park of Detroit has 795 points but will not play long enough to catch Orr. Denis Potvin has a chance. He began this season with 747 career points.

Paul Coffey

Orr's record: 102 assists in a single season
Safe for a long time. Paul Coffey had 67 assists last season. Hockey's highest scoring defencemen average about 50 assists per season. Until Gretzky came along, 102 was the record for forwards and defencemen.

Orr's record: 645 career assists
Brad Park's career assist total at the end of the 1982-83 season stood at 600. Orr's record is in jeopardy if Park's knees hold out a while longer. Denis Potvin of the Islanders is also closing in. Potvin began this season with 528 career assists.

Orr's record: 270 career goals
On some lists, Red Kelly is named as the all-time leading goal scorer among defencemen, but Kelly played much of his time at centre. Potvin (12 goals last season) has an excellent chance of over-taking Orr. He began this season with 219 goals.

While some of Orr's records may topple in time, at least one will endure. Among the young Turks of the blueline—players like Paul Coffey, Dave Babych, Phil Housley, Ray Bourque, Mark Howe and others—is there anyone likely to score 100 points or more for six straight seasons? Orr did it with point totals of 120, 139, 117, 101, 122 and 135.

What's more, he set all his records while skating on knees that had felt the surgeon's knife half a dozen times.

WILL WE EVER BEAT THE SOVIETS?

Not again! That was the reaction from most Canadians when the powerful Soviets skated off with another world hockey championship last spring in Munich, West Germany. The Soviet smoothies walloped Team Canada 8-2 in the final game, capturing the gold medal for the 19th time in the past 23 tournaments. Team Canada won the bronze medal for third place, behind Czechoslovakia. Canada has not finished on top of the world championships since the Trail Smoke Eaters accomplished the feat in 1961.

Once again the question is raised: Will we ever beat the Soviets again, and if so, how?

Paul Reinhart, one of Team Canada's best players in the humiliating 8-2 defeat, said, "I'm still not willing to concede they're better—not until we can go through a season with a forty-five game schedule and have the same team playing together all the time and then go to the world championships. They're a great team. But we're proud to be Canadian players."

Even though there's no clear-cut method for beating the Soviets, most players who participate in tournament play against them say they enjoy the experience.

"It was an honour to be asked to play," said Vancouver's Doug Halward. "It was a real chance for me to play against the best players in the world."

YOU'VE GOT THE WHISTLE, YOU MAKE THE CALL

Many young fans follow the game closely and are proud of their hockey knowledge. But let's pretend you are asked to referee a big-league game. What would you do in the following situations?

1. The goal tender breaks his stick and continues to play with the broken part. Do you give him a penalty?

2. Play stops and one of the players says, "Wait a second, ref. My laces are undone." He sits down on the ice to tie them. What do you do?

3. The pressure is on so the goalie deliberately shoots the puck over the glass and into the crowd. Do you give him a penalty?

4. The puck is loose in the crease and a player from the defending team falls on it. What's the call?

5. A player fails to score on a penalty shot. Where does the ensuing face-off take place?

ANSWERS

1. No. The goal tender is the only player allowed to play with a broken stick.

2. You give him a minor penalty for delay of game.

3. You give him a minor penalty for delay of game.

4. If the puck is in the crease and a defending player falls on it, you call for a penalty shot by the non-offending team.

5. On a failed penalty shot, the ensuing face-off takes place in one of the face-off circles near the goal, in the zone in which the penalty shot was tried.

NHL referees tell me that many big-league players aren't familiar with all the rules. Chances are you did as well on the above quiz as many of them will do. If you got four out of five correct, you really know your hockey.

GOALS AND GOALIES: WHAT ARE THE RULES?

1. Why is there a red light and a green light above the goal at each end?

2. How is a goal determined?

3. If a puck hits the goal post, is it considered a shot on goal?

4. If a goal results from a shot, is it still considered to be a shot on goal?

5. If the puck strikes an official and is deflected into the net, does it count as a goal?

6. What happens in the case of a team already playing shorthanded and the referee signals another minor penalty against that team, but before the whistle is blown, the non-offending team scores?

7. Can a player score by kicking the puck?

8. If a team pulls its goal tender on a delayed penalty, can a goal possibly be scored against that team?

9. If a goalie, in catching the puck, brings his catching hand in back of the goal line, is it ruled as a goal?

10. Have more than two players ever received assists on a goal?

11. Who determines the goals and assists in a game?

ANSWERS

1. The red light is turned on to signal a goal. The green light is used to signal the end of a period or game. A goal cannot be scored when the green light is on.

2. The puck must cross completely over the red goal line, either along the ice or into the area below the crossbar. In other words, the puck may be three-quarters of the way inside the goal but will not constitute a score.

3. No. The NHL reasons that the shot wasn't good enough to score, so it shouldn't count as a shot on goal.

4. Yes. All scoring shots are shots on goal.

5. No. The goal would not be allowed.

6. The goal will be allowed, the penalty or penalties signalled will be washed out and the first of the minor penalties already being served will automatically terminate.

7. Sometimes. A goal counts when a skater kicks the puck and it deflects into the net off any player of the defending side, other than the goalkeeper.

8. Yes, if the puck is accidentally shot, pushed or deflected into the empty goal by a player of the non-offending team.

9. Yes. If the goal judge sees the goalie's glove, with the puck in it, completely cross the goal line he should signal a goal.

10. There was a time when three assists could be awarded on a goal. There was also a time when only one assist could be given. For many years now the greatest number of assists possible has been two.

11. The referee reports to the official scorer the name or number of the player who scored; the official scorer then determines who should be credited with assists.

HOCKEY QUIZ

1. Which team finished the 1982-83 season with the most points?

2. Who won the individual scoring title in 1982-83?

3. This player finished second in the individual scoring race in 1982-83. Who was he?

4. Which Patrick Division team made the Stanley Cup playoffs for the first time in 1982-83?

5. Which of the following teams has never won the Stanley Cup?
   a. Chicago   b. Detroit   c. Philadelphia
   d. St. Louis

6. Who holds the record for the most regular season goals in a single NHL season? How many goals did he score?

7. Only one NHL goalie has ever been credited with scoring a goal in regular season NHL play. Who is he?

8. What country won the gold medal at the Lake Placid Olympics in 1980?

9. How much does a hockey puck weigh?
   a. 100 g   b. 170 g   c. 450 g   d. 50 kg

10. Which of these men was president of the
    NHL for over 30 years?
    a. Harold Ballard   b. Clarence Campbell
    c. Conn Smythe   d. Abraham Lincoln

ANSWERS

1. Boston (with 110 points)

2. Wayne Gretzky

3. Peter Stastny

4. Washington

5. St. Louis

6. Wayne Gretzky with 92 goals in 81-82

7. Bill Smith of the Islanders

8. U.S.A.

9. 170 g

10. Clarence Campbell

NHL STATISTICS: 1982-83

Code: GP—games played; G—goals; A—assists; Pts—points.

PLAYERS	GP	G	A	Pts

CHICAGO

	GP	G	A	Pts
Denis Savard	78	35	85	120
Steve Larmer	80	43	47	90
Al Secord	80	54	32	86
Doug Wilson	74	18	51	69
Darryl Sutter	80	31	30	61
Tom Lysiak	61	23	38	61
Rich Preston	79	25	28	53
Doug Crossman	80	13	40	53
Bill Gardner	77	15	25	40
Bob Murray	79	7	32	39
Curt Fraser	74	12	20	32
Keith Brown	50	4	27	31
Steve Ludzik	66	6	19	25
Tim Higgins	64	14	9	23
Rick Paterson	79	14	9	23
Peter Marsh	68	6	14	20
Dave Feamster	78	6	12	18
Denis Cyr	52	8	9	17
Troy Murray	54	8	8	16
Greg Fox	76	0	13	13
Jack O'Callahan	39	0	11	11
Mike Fidler	4	2	1	3
Murray Bannerman	41	0	1	1
Jerome Dupont	1	0	0	0
Grant Mulvey	3	0	0	0
Tony Esposito	39	0	0	0

MINNESOTA

	GP	G	A	Pts
Neal Broten	79	32	45	77
Bobby Smith	77	24	53	77
Tom McCarthy	80	28	48	76
Dino Ciccarelli	77	37	38	75
Steve Payne	80	30	39	69
Brian Bellows	78	35	30	65
Craig Hartsburg	78	12	50	62
Tim Young	70	18	35	53
Gordie Roberts	80	3	41	44
Willi Plett	71	25	14	39
Brad Maxwell	77	11	28	39
Al MacAdam	73	11	22	33
Mike Eaves	75	16	16	32
Jordy Douglas	68	13	14	27
Curt Giles	76	2	21	23
George Ferguson	72	8	12	20
Ron Friest	50	6	7	13
Gary Sargent	18	3	6	9
Dan Mandich	67	3	4	7
Fred Barrett	51	1	3	4
Warren Young	4	1	1	2
Don Beaupre	36	0	2	2
Gilles Meloche	47	0	2	1
Bob Bergloff	2	0	0	0
Randy Velischek	3	0	0	0
Wes Jarvis	3	0	0	0
Dave Richter	6	0	0	0

TORONTO

	GP	G	A	Pts		GP	G	A	Pts
John Anderson	80	31	49	80	Normand Aubin	26	4	1	5
Rick Vaive	78	51	28	79	Fred Boimistruck	26	2	3	5
Peter Ihnacak	80	28	38	66	Russ Adam	8	1	2	3
Walt Poddubny	72	28	31	59	Gary Nylund	16	0	3	3
Miroslav Frycer	67	25	30	55	Mike Palmateer	53	0	3	3
Dan Daoust	52	18	34	52	Serge Boisvert	17	0	2	2
Borje Salming	69	7	38	45	Dave Shand	1	0	1	1
Bill Derlogo	58	13	24	37	Craig Muni	2	0	1	1
Gaston Gingras	67	11	26	37	Marc Magnan	4	1	0	1
Greg Terrion	74	16	16	32	Reid Bailey	1	0	0	0
Bill Harris	76	11	19	30	Bob Parent	1	0	0	0
Jim Korn	80	8	21	29	Vincent Tremblay	1	0	0	0
Dave Farrish	56	4	24	28	Rod Willard	1	0	0	0
Terry Martin	76	14	13	27	Ken Strong	2	0	0	0
Jim Benning	74	5	17	22	Gary Yaremchuk	3	0	0	0
Frank Nigro	51	6	15	21	Leigh Verstraete	3	0	0	0
Mike Kaszycki	22	1	13	14	Rocky Saganiuk	3	0	0	0
Stewart Gavin	63	6	5	11	Paul Higgins	22	0	0	0
Slava Duris	32	2	8	10	Bob McGill	30	0	0	0
Barry Melrose	52	2	5	7	Rick St. Croix	33	0	0	0

ST. LOUIS

Bernie Federko	75	24	60	84
Brian Sutter	79	46	30	76
Jorgen Pettersson	75	35	38	73
Blake Dunlop	78	22	44	66
Rob Ramage	78	16	35	51
Perry Turnbull	79	32	15	47
Joe Mullen	49	17	30	47
Wayne Babych	71	16	23	39
Alain Lemieux	42	9	25	34
Andre Dore	77	5	27	32
Guy Lapointe	54	3	23	26
Mike Zuke	43	8	16	24
Jack Brownschidle	72	1	22	23
Larry Patey	67	9	12	21
Mark Reeds	20	5	14	19
Blair Chapman	39	7	11	18
Mike Crombeen	80	6	11	17
Tim Bothwell	61	4	11	15
Bobby Crawford	27	5	9	14
Rik Wilson	56	3	11	14
Jack Carlson	54	6	1	7
Perry Anderson	18	5	2	7
Ed Kea	46	0	5	5
Alain Vigneault	28	1	3	4
Jim Pavese	24	0	2	2
Ralph Klassen	29	0	2	2
Curt Brackenbury	6	1	0	1
Pat Hickey	1	0	0	0
Rob Tudor	2	0	0	0
Rick Heinz	9	0	0	0
Bill Stewart	7	0	0	0
Garry Hart	8	0	0	0
Mike Liut	68	0	0	0

EDMONTON

Wayne Gretzky	80	71	125	196
Mark Messier	77	48	58	106
Glenn Anderson	72	48	56	104
Jari Kurri	80	45	59	104
Paul Coffey	80	29	67	96
Ken Linseman	72	33	42	75
Charlie Huddy	76	20	37	57
Willy Lindstrom	73	26	30	56
Pat Hughes	80	25	20	45
Tom Roulston	67	19	21	40
Kevin Lowe	80	6	34	40
Dave Lumley	72	13	24	37
Jaroslav Pouzar	74	15	18	33
Dave Hunter	80	13	18	31
Randy Gregg	80	6	22	28
Dave Semenko	75	12	15	27
Lee Fogolin	72	0	18	18
Marc Habscheid	32	3	10	13
Don Jackson	71	2	8	10
Andy Moog	50	0	4	4
John Blum	5	0	3	3
Garry Unger	16	2	0	2
Garry Lariviere	17	0	2	2
L. Middlebrook	10	0	1	1
Todd Strueby	1	0	0	0
Don Nachbaur	4	0	0	0
Grant Fuhr	32	0	0	0

DETROIT

John Ogrodnick	80	41	44	85
Reed Larson	80	22	52	74
Danny Gare	79	26	35	61
Ivan Boldirev	2	18	37	55
Mark Osborne	80	19	24	43
Walt McKechnie	64	14	29	43
Willy Huber	74	14	29	43
Mike Blaisdell	80	18	23	41
Dwight Foster	62	17	22	39
Paul Woods	63	13	20	33
Reggie Leach	78	15	17	32
Greg Smith	73	4	26	30
Stan Weir	57	5	24	29
Tom Rowe	51	6	10	16
John Barrett	79	4	10	14
Mark Lofthouse	28	8	4	12
Derek Smith	42	7	4	11
Murray Craven	31	4	7	11
Jim Schoenfeld	57	1	10	11
Colin Campbell	53	1	7	8
Kelly Kisio	15	4	3	7
Ken Solheim	35	2	4	6
Randy Ladouceur	27	0	4	4
Joe Paterson	33	2	1	3
Gilles Gilbert	20	0	3	3
Bobby Francis	14	2	0	2
Claude Loiselle	18	2	0	2
Larry Trader	15	0	2	2
Dennis Polonich	11	0	1	1
Corrado Micalef	34	0	1	1
Jim Rutherford	1	0	0	0
Brad Smith	1	0	0	0
Bobby Crawford	1	0	0	0
Greg Joly	2	0	0	0
Greg Stefan	35	0	0	0

WINNIPEG

Dale Hawerchuk	79	40	51	91
Paul MacLean	80	32	44	76
Dave Babych	79	3	61	74
Thomas Steen	75	26	33	59
Lucien Deblois	79	27	27	54
Brian Mullen	80	24	26	50
Dave Christian	55	18	26	44
Doug Smail	80	15	29	44
Morris Lukowich	69	22	21	43
Bengt Lundholm	58	14	28	42
Laurie Boschman	74	11	17	28
Normand Dupont	39	7	16	23
Tim Watters	77	5	18	23
Bryan Maxwell	54	7	13	20
Serge Savard	76	4	16	20
Scott Arniel	75	13	5	18
Don Spring	80	0	16	16
Ron Wilson	12	6	3	9
Craig Levie	22	4	5	9
Moe Mantha	21	2	7	9
Murray Eaves	26	2	7	9
Larry Hopkins	12	3	1	4
Wade Campbell	42	1	2	3
Ed Staniowski	17	0	1	1
Brian Hayward	24	0	1	1
Jimmy Mann	40	0	1	1
Doug Soetaert	44	0	1	1

VANCOUVER

Stan Smyl	74	38	50	88
Thomas Gradin	80	32	54	86
Darcy Rota	73	42	39	81
Ivan Hlinka	65	19	44	63
Doug Halward	75	19	33	52
Rick Lanz	74	10	38	48
Patrik Sundstrom	74	23	23	46
Kevin McCarthy	74	12	28	40
Lars Molin	58	12	27	39
Jiri Bubla	72	2	28	30
Gary Lupul	40	18	10	28
Jim Nill	65	7	15	22
Dave Williams	68	8	13	21
Moe Lemay	44	11	9	20
Lars Lindgren	64	6	14	20
Tony Tanti	40	9	8	17
Ron Delorme	56	5	8	13
Mark Kirton	41	5	7	12
Harold Snepts	46	2	8	10
Marc Crawford	41	4	5	9
Blair MacDonald	17	3	4	7
Neil Belland	14	2	4	6
Gerry Minor	39	1	5	6
Stuart Kulak	4	1	1	2
Tony Currie	8	1	1	2
John Garrett	34	0	2	2
Richard Brodeur	58	0	1	1
Frank Caprice	1	0	0	0
Michel Petit	2	0	0	0
Ken Ellacott	12	0	0	0

CALGARY

Kent Nilsson	80	46	58	104
Lanny McDonald	80	66	32	98
Paul Reinhart	78	17	58	75
Guy Chouinard	80	13	59	72
Doug Risebrough	71	21	37	58
Mel Bridgman	79	19	31	50
Kari Eloranta	80	4	40	44
Jim Peplinski	80	15	26	41
Kevin Lavallee	60	19	16	35
Jamie Hislop	79	14	19	33
Phil Russell	78	13	18	31
Eddy Beers	41	11	15	26
Dave Hindmarch	60	11	12	23
Jim Jackson	48	8	12	20
Steve Christoff	45	9	8	17
Steve Konroyd	79	4	13	17
Richie Dunn	80	3	11	14
Carl Mokosak	41	7	6	13
Kari Jalonen	25	9	3	12
Greg Meredith	35	5	4	9
Charles Bourgeois	15	2	3	5
Jamie Macoun	22	1	4	5
Rejean Lemelin	39	0	5	5
Al MacInnis	14	1	3	4
Pierre Rioux	14	1	2	3
Tim Hunter	16	1	0	1
Pat Ribble	28	0	1	1
Don Edwards	39	0	1	1
Mike Vernon	2	0	0	0
Howard Walker	3	0	0	0
Tim Harrer	3	0	0	0
Gord Hampson	4	0	0	0
Tim Bernhardt	6	0	0	0

LOS ANGELES

Marcel Dionne	80	56	51	107
Charlie Simmer	80	29	51	80
Jim Fox	77	28	40	68
Larry Murphy	77	14	48	62
Dave Taylor	46	21	37	58
Bernie Nicholls	71	28	22	50
Terry Ruskowski	76	14	32	46
Daryl Evans	80	18	22	40
Mark Hardy	74	5	34	39
John Paul Kelly	65	16	15	31
Jerry Korab	72	3	26	29
Mike Murphy	74	16	11	27
Steve Bozek	53	13	13	26
Warren Holmes	39	8	16	24
Doug Smith	42	11	11	22
Ulf Isaksson	50	7	15	22
Dean Hopkins	49	5	12	17
Jay Wells	69	3	12	15
Dave Lewis	79	2	10	12
Dean Kennedy	55	0	12	12
Dave Morrison	24	3	3	6
Howard Scruton	4	0	4	4
Brian MacLellan	8	0	3	3
Phil Sykes	7	2	0	2
Don Bonar	20	1	1	2
Scott Gruhl	7	0	2	2
Markus Mattsson	21	0	2	2
Victor Nechaev	3	1	0	1
Pierre Giroux	6	1	0	1
Jim Brown	3	0	1	1
Doug Keans	6	0	1	1
Peter Helander	7	0	1	1
Mario Lessard	19	0	1	1
Gary Laskoski	46	1	1	1
Blair Barnes	1	0	0	0
Al Sims	1	0	0	0
Bob Gladney	1	0	0	0
Rick Blight	2	0	0	0
Dean Turner	3	0	0	0
Dave Gans	3	0	0	0
Mike Blake	9	0	0	0

120

BOSTON

	GP	G	A	Pts
Barry Pederson	77	46	61	107
Rick Middleton	80	49	47	96
Keith Crowder	74	35	39	74
Peter McNab	74	22	52	74
Ray Bourque	65	22	51	73
Mike Krushelnyski	79	23	42	65
Tom Fergus	80	28	35	63
Mike O'Connell	80	14	39	53
Bruce Crowder	80	21	19	40
Brad Park	76	10	26	36
Craig MacTavish	75	10	20	30
Luc Dufour	73	14	11	25
Mike Milbury	78	9	15	24
Terry O'Reilly	19	6	14	20
Brad Palmer	73	6	11	17
Wayne Cashman	65	4	11	15
Marty Howe	78	1	11	12
Randy Hillier	70	0	10	10
Normand Leveille	9	3	6	9
Steve Kasper	24	2	6	8
Gord Kluzak	70	1	6	7
Dave Barr	10	1	1	2
Pete Peeters	62	0	2	2
Mike Gillis	5	0	1	1
Larry Melnyk	1	0	0	0
Scott McLellan	2	0	0	0
Marco Baron	9	0	0	0
Mike Moffat	13	0	0	0

BUFFALO

	GP	G	A	Pts
Gilbert Perreault	77	30	46	76
Tony McKegney	78	36	37	73
Phil Housley	77	19	47	66
Dale McCourt	62	20	32	52
Mike Foligno	66	22	25	47
Gilles Hamel	66	22	20	42
Ric Seiling	75	19	22	41
Andre Savard	68	16	25	41
Mike Ramsay	77	8	30	38
Dave Andreychuk	43	14	23	37
Hannu Virta	74	13	24	37
Brent Peterson	75	13	24	37
Lindy Ruff	60	12	17	29
Craig Ramsey	64	11	18	29
Paul Cyr	36	15	12	27
John Van Boxmeer	65	6	21	27
Sean McKenna	46	10	14	24
Steve Patrick	56	9	13	22
Mal Davis	24	8	12	20
Mike Moller	49	6	12	18
Larry Playfair	79	4	13	17
Bill Hait	72	3	12	15
Dave Fenyves	24	0	8	8
J.F. Sauve	9	0	4	4
G. Robertson	5	1	2	3
Gary McAdam	4	1	0	1
Bob Sauve	54	0	1	1
Kari Suikkanen	1	0	0	0
Ron Fischer	3	0	0	0
Jere Gillis	3	0	0	0
Phil Myre	5	0	0	0
Jacques Cloutier	25	0	0	0

MONTREAL

	GP	G	A	Pts
Guy Lafleur	68	27	49	76
Ryan Walter	80	29	46	75
Mats Naslund	74	26	45	71
Mark Napier	73	40	27	67
Mario Tremblay	80	30	37	67
Pierre Mondou	76	29	37	66
Larry Robinson	71	14	49	63
Steve Shutt	78	35	22	57
Doug Wickenheiser	78	25	30	55
Keith Acton	78	24	26	50
Guy Carbonneau	77	18	29	47
Robert Picard	64	7	31	38
Gilbert Delorme	78	12	21	33
Bob Gainey	80	12	18	30
Rick Green	66	2	24	26
Craig Ludwig	80	0	25	25
Mark Hunter	31	8	8	16
Chris Nilan	66	6	8	14
Rejean Houle	16	2	3	5
Bill Root	46	2	3	5
Ric Nattress	40	1	3	4
Richard Sevigny	38	0	1	1
Rick Wamsley	46	0	1	1
Yvan Joly	1	0	0	0
Mark Holden	2	0	0	0
Dwight Schofield	2	0	0	0
Bill Kitchen	8	0	0	0

QUEBEC

	GP	G	A	Pts
Peter Stastny	75	47	77	124
Michel Goulet	80	57	48	105
Anton Stastny	79	32	60	92
Marian Stastny	60	36	43	79
Real Cloutier	68	28	39	67
Wilf Paiement	80	26	38	64
Dale Hunter	80	17	46	63
Marc Tardif	76	21	31	52
Alain Cote	79	12	28	40
Louis Sleigher	51	14	10	24
Dave Pichette	53	3	21	24
Jacques Richard	35	9	14	23
Normand Rochefort	62	6	17	23
Pierre Aubry	77	7	9	16
Wally Weir	58	7	9	16
Andre Dupont	46	3	12	15
Pat Price	52	2	13	15
Mario Marois	36	2	12	14
Randy Moller	75	2	12	14
Blake Wesley	74	4	9	13
Rick Lapointe	43	2	9	11
Jean Hamel	51	2	7	9
Tim Tookey	12	1	6	7
Richard David	16	3	3	6
Anders Eldebrink	17	2	3	5
Don Bouchard	50	0	4	4
Basil McRae	22	1	1	2
Paul Gillis	7	0	2	2
Dennis Sobchuk	2	1	0	1
Jean Gaulin	1	0	0	0
Mike Eagles	2	0	0	0
David Shaw	2	0	0	0
Terry Johnson	3	0	0	0
Gaston Therrien	5	0	0	0
Michel Bolduc	7	0	0	0

HARTFORD

Ron Francis	79	31	59	90
Blaine Stoughton	72	45	31	76
Mark Johnson	73	31	38	69
Ray Neufeld	80	26	31	57
Doug Sullivan	77	22	19	41
Pierre Larouche	38	18	22	40
Bob Sullivan	62	18	19	37
Pierre Lacroix	69	6	30	36
Marlin Malinowski	80	8	25	33
Mark Renaud	77	3	28	31
Chris Kotsopoulos	68	6	24	30
Risto Siltanen	74	5	25	30
Greg Adams	79	10	13	23
Mike McDougal	55	8	10	18
Mickey Volcan	68	4	13	17
Paul Lawless	47	6	9	15
Warren Miller	56	1	10	11
George Lyle	16	4	6	10
Ed Hospodar	72	1	9	10
Michel Galarneau	38	5	4	9
Russ Anderson	57	0	6	6
Don Fridgen	11	2	2	4
Archie Henderson	15	2	1	3
Paul Marshall	13	1	2	3
Greg Millen	60	0	2	2
Stuart Smith	18	1	0	1
Randy Gilhen	2	0	1	1
Mike Hoffman	2	0	1	1
Mark Paterson	2	0	0	0
Jeff Brownschidle	4	0	0	0
Paul MacDermid	7	0	0	0
Mike Veisor	23	0	0	0

N.Y. ISLANDERS

Mike Bossy	79	60	58	118
Bryan Trottier	80	34	55	89
John Tonelli	76	31	40	71
Denis Potvin	69	12	54	66
Bob Bourne	77	20	42	62
Tomas Jonsson	72	13	35	48
Clark Gillies	70	21	20	41
Brent Sutter	80	21	19	40
Butch Goring	75	19	20	39
Duane Sutter	75	13	19	32
Bob Nystrom	74	10	20	30
Stefan Persson	70	4	25	29
Dave Langevin	73	4	17	21
Greg Gilbert	45	8	11	19
Ken Morrow	79	5	11	16
Wayne Merrick	59	4	12	16
Mats Hallin	30	7	7	14
Anders Kallur	55	6	8	14
Mike McEwen	42	2	11	13
Billy Carroll	71	1	11	12
Paul Boutilier	29	4	5	9
Gord Lane	44	3	4	7
Roland Melanson	44	0	3	3
Kevin Devine	2	0	1	1
Gord Dineen	2	0	0	0
Darcy Regier	6	0	0	0
Billy Smith	41	0	0	0

PHILADELPHIA

Bobby Clarke	80	23	62	85
Darryl Sittler	80	43	40	83
Brian Propp	80	40	42	82
Mark Howe	76	20	47	67
Ron Flockhart	73	29	31	60
Bill Barber	66	27	33	60
Ray Allison	67	21	30	51
Ilkka Sinisalo	61	21	29	50
Poul Holmgren	77	19	24	43
Lindsay Carson	78	18	19	37
Miroslav Dvorak	80	4	33	37
Mark Taylor	61	8	25	33
Behn Wilson	62	8	24	32
Paul Evans	58	8	20	28
Brad McCrimmon	79	4	21	25
Glen Cochrane	77	2	22	24
Tim Kerr	24	11	8	19
Tom Gorence	53	7	7	14
Bob Hoffmeyer	35	2	11	13
Brad Marsh	68	2	11	13
Frank Bathe	57	1	8	9
Dave Michayluk	13	2	6	8
Pelle Lindbergh	40	0	4	4
John Paddock	10	2	1	3
Dan Poulin	2	2	0	2
Andy Brickley	3	1	1	2
Ron Sutter	10	1	1	2
Bob Froese	24	0	2	2
Ross Fitzpatrick	1	0	0	0
Gordie Williams	1	0	0	0
Dave Brown	2	0	0	0
Michel Larocque	16	0	0	0

WASHINGTON

Dennis Maruk	80	31	50	81
Mike Gartner	73	38	38	76
Bobby Carpenter	80	32	37	69
Bengt Gustaffson	67	22	42	64
Alan Haworth	74	23	27	50
Milan Novy	73	18	30	48
Craig Laughlin	75	17	27	44
Bob Gould	80	22	18	40
Ken Houston	71	25	14	39
Glen Currie	68	11	28	39
Gaetan Duchesne	77	18	19	37
Greg Theberge	70	8	28	36
Rod Langway	80	3	29	32
Doug Jarvis	80	8	22	30
Brian Engblom	73	5	22	27
Scott Stevens	77	9	16	25
Timo Blomqvist	61	1	17	18
Chris Valentine	23	7	10	17
Ted Bulley	39	4	9	13
Darren Veitch	10	0	8	8
Randy Holt	70	0	8	8
Paul Mackinnon	19	2	2	4
Torrie Robertson	5	2	0	2
Lee Norwood	8	0	1	1
Eric Calder	1	0	0	0
Robbie Moore	1	0	0	0
Dave Parro	6	0	0	0
Doug Hicks	6	0	0	0
Pat Riggin	38	0	0	0
Al Jensen	40	0	0	0

N.Y. RANGERS

Mike Rogers	71	29	47	76
Mark Pavelich	78	37	38	75
Don Maloney	78	29	40	69
R. Ruotsalainen	77	16	53	69
Anders Hedberg	78	25	34	59
Mikko Leinonen	78	17	34	51
Dave Maloney	78	8	42	50
Rob McClanahan	78	22	26	48
Ron Duguay	72	19	25	44
Ed Johnstone	52	15	21	36
Barry Beck	66	12	22	34
V. Nedomansky	57	14	17	31
Robbie Ftorek	61	12	19	31
K. E. Andersson	71	8	20	28
Nick Fotiu	72	8	13	21
Mike Allison	39	11	9	20
Bill Baker	70	4	14	18
Chris Kontos	44	8	7	15
Rick Chartraw	57	5	7	12
Scot Kleinendorst	30	2	9	11
Tom Laidlaw	80	0	10	10
Ron Greschner	10	3	5	8
Ulf Nilsson	10	2	4	6
Mike Backman	7	1	3	4
Ed Mio	41	0	3	3
Dave Silk	16	1	1	2
Steve Weeks	18	0	2	2
Pat Conacher	5	0	1	1
Cam Connor	1	0	0	0
John Davidson	2	0	0	0
Steve Baker	3	0	0	0
Graeme Nicolson	10	0	0	0
Glen Hanlon	35	0	0	0

NEW JERSEY

Aaron Broten	73	16	39	55
Don Lever	79	23	30	53
Bob MacMillan	71	19	29	48
Tapio Levo	73	7	40	47
Jeff Larmer	65	21	24	45
Hector Marini	77	17	28	45
Steve Tambellini	73	25	18	43
Brent Ashton	76	14	19	33
Rick Meagher	61	15	14	29
Paul Gagne	53	14	15	29
Murray Brumwell	59	5	14	19
Jan Ludvig	51	7	10	17
Joel Quenneville	74	5	12	17
Mike Antonovich	30	7	7	14
Glenn Merkosky	34	4	10	14
Bob Lorimer	66	3	10	13
Mike Kitchen	77	4	8	12
Yvon Vautour	52	4	7	11
Rob Palmer	60	1	10	11
Dave Cameron	35	5	4	9
John Wensink	42	2	7	9
Carol Vadnais	51	2	7	9
Pat Verbeek	6	3	2	5
Dave Hutchison	32	1	4	5
Garry Howatt	38	1	4	5
Jukka Porvari	8	1	3	4
Glenn Resch	65	0	3	3
Larry Floyd	5	1	0	1
Joe Cirella	2	0	1	1
Mike Moher	9	0	1	1
Ron Low	14	0	1	1
Randy Pierce	3	0	0	0
Shawn MacKenzie	6	0	0	0

PITTSBURGH

Doug Shedden	80	24	43	67
Rick Kehoe	75	29	36	65
Greg Malone	80	17	44	61
Pat Boutette	80	27	29	56
Randy Carlyle	61	15	41	56
Paul Gardner	70	28	27	55
Mike Bullard	57	22	22	44
Dave Hannan	74	11	22	33
Paul Baxter	75	11	21	32
Greg Hotham	58	2	30	32
Peter Lee	63	13	13	26
Andre St. Laurent	70	13	9	22
Anders Hakansson	67	9	12	21
Randy Boyd	56	4	14	18
Steve Gatzos	44	6	7	13
Kevin McClelland	38	5	4	9

Gary Rissling	40	5	4	9
Marc Chorney	67	3	5	8
Ron Meighan	41	2	6	8
Tony Feltrin	32	3	3	6
Pat Graham	20	1	5	6
Tim Hrynewich	30	2	3	5
Doug Lecuyer	12	1	4	5
Rick MacLeish	6	0	5	5
Rod Buskas	41	2	2	4
Stan Jonathan	20	0	3	3
Jim Hamilton	5	0	2	2
Michel Dion	49	0	2	2
Bobby Simpson	4	1	0	1
Denis Herron	31	0	1	1

GOAL TENDERS

Goal tender	GP	Mi	Avg	W	L	T	EN	SO	GA	SA	Pct
N.Y. ISLANDERS											
Roland Melanson	44	2460	2.66	24	12	5	3	1	109	1206	.909
Billy Smith	41	2340	2.87	18	14	7	2	1	112	1195	.906
Totals	80	4800	2.83	42	26	12	—	2	226	2401	.906
BOSTON											
Pete Peters	62	3611	2.36	40	11	9	2	8	142	1482	.904
Marco Baron	9	516	3.84	6	3	0	1	0	33	233	.858
Mike Moffat	13	673	4.37	4	6	1	1	0	49	271	.819
Totals	80	4800	2.85	50	20	10	—	8	228	1986	.885
PHILADELPHIA											
Bob Froese	24	1406	2.52	17	4	2	0	4	59	569	.896
Pelle Lindbergh	40	2334	2.98	23	13	3	2	3	116	1060	.890
Rick St. Croix	16	940	3.45	9	5	2	1	0	54	432	.875
Michel Larocque	2	120	4.00	0	1	1	0	0	8	56	.857
Totals	80	4800	3.00	49	23	8	—	7	240	2117	.887
CHICAGO											
Murray Bannerman	41	2460	3.10	24	12	5	2	4	127	1283	.901
Tony Esposito	39	2340	3.46	23	11	5	4	1	135	1203	.887
Totals	80	4800	3.35	47	23	10	—	5	268	2486	892
WASHINGTON											
Robbie Moore	1	20	3.00	0	1	0	1	0	1	8	.857
Pat Riggin	38	2161	3.36	17	9	9	4	0	121	1015	.880
Al Jensen	40	2358	3.44	21	12	6	1	1	135	1140	.881
Dave Parro	6	261	4.37	1	3	1	1	0	19	127	.849
Totals	80	4800	3.54	39	25	16	—	1	283	2290	.876
BUFFALO											
Bob Sauve	54	3110	3.45	25	20	7	3	1	179	1393	.871
Jacques Cloutier	25	1390	3.50	10	7	6	0	0	81	572	.858
Phil Myre	5	300	4.20	3	2	0	1	0	21	152	.861
Totals	80	4800	3.56	38	29	13	—	1	285	2117	.865
MONTREAL											
Richard Sevigny	38	2130	3.44	15	11	8	5	1	122	1045	.883
Rick Wamsley	46	2583	3.51	27	12	5	2	0	151	1240	.878
Mark Holden	2	87	4.14	0	1	1	0	0	6	42	.857
Totals	80	4800	3.58	42	24	14	—	1	286	2327	.877
N.Y. RANGERS											
John Davidson	2	120	2.50	1	1	0	0	0	5	55	.909
Steve Baker	3	102	2.94	0	1	0	2	0	5	44	.881
Glen Hanlon	21	1173	3.43	9	10	1	1	0	67	635	.894
Ed Mio	41	2365	3.45	16	18	6	33	2	136	1159	.882
Steve Weeks	18	1040	3.92	9	5	3	0	0	68	491	.862
Totals	80	4800	3.59	35	35	10	—	2	287	2384	.880
MINNESOTA											
Gilles Meloche	47	2689	3.57	20	13	11	2	1	160	1411	.886
Don Beaupre	36	2011	3.58	19	10	5	2	0	120	1048	.885
Markus Mattsson	2	100	3.60	1	1	0	0	1	6	70	.914
Totals	80	4800	3.63	40	24	16	—	2	290	2529	.885
VANCOUVER											
John Garrett	17	934	3.08	7	6	3	2	1	48	506	.905
Richard Brodeur	58	3291	3.79	21	26	8	6	0	208	1641	.873
Ken Ellacott	12	555	4.43	2	3	4	1	0	41	309	.867
Frank Caprice	1	20	9.00	0	0	0	0	0	3	8	.625
Totals	80	4800	3.86	30	35	15	—	1	309	2464	.875
EDMONTON											
L. Middlebrook	1	60	3.00	1	0	0	0	0	3	33	.909
Andy Moog	50	2833	3.54	33	8	7	1	1	167	1531	.891
Grant Fuhr	32	1803	4.29	13	12	5	4	0	129	974	.867
Ron Low	3	104	5.77	0	1	0	1	0	10	55	.815
Totals	80	4800	3.94	47	21	12	—	1	315	2593	.879

GOAL TENDERS

Goal tender	GP	Mi	Avg	W	L	T	EN	SO	GA	SA	Pct
ST. LOUIS											
Mike Liut	68	3794	3.72	21	27	13	4	1	235	1922	.877
Rick Heinz	9	335	4.30	1	5	1	1	1	24	158	.847
Glen Hanlon	14	671	4.47	3	8	1	2	0	50	414	.879
Totals	80	4800	3.95	25	40	15	—	2	316	2494	.873
CALGARY											
Rejean Lemelin	39	2211	3.61	16	12	8	3	0	133	1192	.888
Don Edwards	39	2209	4.02	16	15	6	1	1	148	1255	.882
Tim Bernhardt	6	280	4.50	0	5	0	0	0	21	147	.857
Mike Vernon	2	100	6.60	0	2	0	0	0	11	46	.761
Totals	80	4800	3.96	32	34	14	—	1	317	2640	.880
TORONTO											
Vincent Tremblay	1	40	3.00	0	0	0	0	0	2	27	.976
Bob Parent	1	40	3.00	0	0	0	0	0	2	22	.909
Rick St. Croix	17	920	3.78	4	9	2	0	0	58	508	.886
Mike Palmateer	53	2965	3.99	21	23	7	3	0	197	1534	.871
Michel Larocque	16	835	4.89	3	8	3	0	0	68	454	.850
Totals	80	4800	4.13	28	40	12	—	0	330	2545	.870
WINNIPEG											
Brian Hayward	24	1440	3.71	10	12	2	0	1	89	786	.887
Doug Soetaert	44	2533	4.12	19	19	6	3	0	174	1328	.869
Ed Staniowski	17	827	4.72	4	8	0	2	1	65	417	.843
Totals	80	4800	4.16	33	39	8	—	2	333	2531	.868
QUEBEC											
Don Bouchard	50	2947	4.01	20	21	8	1	1	197	1579	.875
John Garrett	17	953	4.03	2	7	1	1	0	41	344	.880
Clint Malarchuk	15	900	4.73	8	5	2	0	0	71	517	.863
Totals	80	4800	4.20	34	34	12	—	1	336	2603	.871
NEW JERSEY											
Glenn Resch	65	3650	3.98	15	35	12	2	0	242	1933	.875
Ron Low	11	608	4.05	2	7	1	1	0	41	344	.880
L. Middlebrook	9	412	5.39	0	6	1	0	0	37	220	.832
Shawn Mackenzie	6	130	6.92	0	1	0	0	0	15	68	.779
Totals	80	4800	4.23	17	49	14	—	0	338	2565	.868
DETROIT											
Corrado Micalef	34	1756	3.62	11	13	5	5	2	106	766	.861
Gilles Gillert	20	1137	4.49	4	14	1	0	0	85	565	.850
Greg Stefan	35	1847	4.52	6	16	9	2	0	139	947	.853
Jim Rutherford	1	60	7.00	0	1	0	0	0	7	39	.821
Totals	80	4800	4.30	21	44	15	—	2	344	2317	.852
LOS ANGELES											
Mike Blake	9	432	4.17	4	4	0	1	0	30	211	.857
Markus Mattsson	19	899	4.34	5	5	4	1	1	65	454	.857
Gary Laskoski	46	2277	4.56	15	20	4	3	0	173	1212	.857
Mario Lessard	19	888	4.59	3	10	2	0	1	68	432	.843
Doug Keans	6	304	4.74	0	2	2	0	0	24	138	.826
Totals	80	4800	4.56	27	41	12	—	2	365	2447	.851
PITTSBURGH											
Michel Dion	49	2791	4.26	12	30	4	9	0	198	1511	.868
Denis Herron	31	1707	5.31	5	18	5	1	1	151	931	.838
Nick Ricci	3	147	6.53	1	2	0	1	0	16	77	.789
Roberto Romano	3	155	6.97	0	3	0	0	0	18	96	.813
Totals	80	4800	4.93	18	53	9	—	1	394	2615	.849
HARTFORD											
Greg Millen	60	3520	4.81	14	38	6	3	1	282	2056	.863
Mike Veisor	23	1280	5.53	5	16	1	0	1	118	815	.855
Totals	80	4800	5.04	19	54	7	—	2	403	2871	.860

Code—Gi-games played. Mi-minutes played. Ga-goals against. So-shutouts. Av-60 minute average. En-empty net goals.

HOCKEY'S TOP DOZEN ALL-TIME SCORERS

Player	Seasons	Games	Goals
Gord Howe	26	1767	801
Phil Esposito	18	1282	717
Bobby Hull	16	1063	610
John Bucyk	23	1540	556
Maurice Richard	18	978	544
*Marcel Dionne	12	937	544
Stan Mikita	22	1394	541
Frank Mahovlich	18	1181	533
Jean Beliveau	18	1125	507
Jean Ratelle	21	1281	491
Norm Ullman	20	1410	490
*Guy Lafleur	12	862	486

* Active players